SUPER Salad Selection

Mouthwatering recipes for crisp, fresh salads and tasty dressings

SUPER Salad Selection

Mouthwatering recipes for crisp, fresh salads and tasty dressings

Edited by Jane Donovan

APPLE

A QUINTET BOOK

Published by The Apple Press
6 Blundell Street
London N7 9BH

ISBN 1-85076-944-3

This book was designed and produced by
Quintet Publishing Limited
6 Blundell Street
London N7 9BH

Creative Director: Richard Dewing
Art Director: Silke Braun
Designer: John Strange
Project Editor: Clare Hubbard
Editor: Jane Donovan

Typeset in Great Britain by
Central Southern Typesetters, Eastbourne
Manufactured in Hong Kong by
Regent Publishing Services Ltd.
Printed in Hong Kong by
Sing Cheong Printing Co. Ltd.

Material in this publication previously appeared in: *Cajun
Cooking*, Marjie Lambert; *Caribbean Cooking*, Devinia Sookia;
The Complete Rice Cookbook, Myra Street; *Creole Cooking*,
Sue Mullin; *Dressings and Marinades*, Hilaire Walden;
Fabulous Fruit Cookbook, Moya Clarke; *The Fresh Pasta
Cookbook*, Bridget Jones; *The Great Chilli Cookbook*, Gina
Steer; *Great Garlic Cookbook*, Sophie Hale; *Korean Cooking*,
Hilaire Walden; *North African Cooking*, Hilaire Walden; *Nuevo
Cubano Cooking*, Sue Mullin; *Portuguese Cooking*, Hilaire
Walden; *Salads*, Sue Mullin; *Southern Cooking*, Marjie
Lambert; *Spanish Cooking*, Pepita Aris; *Vegetarian Pasta
Cookbook*, Sarah Maxwell.

CONTENTS

INTRODUCTION

I CAN REMEMBER when a salad meant little more than iceberg lettuce, onion, tomato and – if the chef was really creative – some cucumber and grated carrots, usually dressed with oil and vinegar.

The number of foodstuffs stocked in the average supermarket produce section 20 years ago amounted to fewer than 65 items: today, more than 300 ingredients, many of them used in making salads, vie for space in overflowing bins. One of the reasons for this expansion is the relatively recent interest in olive oil. When the top-selling speciality food product at supermarkets became olive oils, it naturally followed that the produce section would blossom with a more international cornucopia of lettuces, herbs, vegetables and fruits. Today, there are so many leaves, sprigs, herbs and other salad ingredients in most supermarkets – not to mention gourmet and ethnic food shops – that some days I feel like toting a botanical guide with me when I go shopping.

We can all rejoice that the crunchy ingredients going into salads are not just trendy; they are also good for our health. Gone are the days when gourmet cooking meant throwing a carton of cream and a bottle of brandy into a stew. We have entered the day of the 'designer greens', as some food writers have called rocket, radicchio and the ever-growing list of salad items, many of which were eaten by ancient Romans and Greeks, but are only now becoming widely popular. And if we want to stay on top of the trend, we need to know our rocket from our courgette, and that radicchio is pronounced *radikio*, not *radicchio*.

Lots of other ingredients are used in salads in addition to greens such as vegetables, fruits, nuts, onions and cheeses, to name but a few and if the ingredient is unusual I will say a word about it with the recipe.

strong flavours. New York food writer Mindy Heiferling calls salads such as Rocket, Radicchio and Endive with Duck Crackling and Warm Sorrel Vinaigrette, which she found on a restaurant menu, 'Nouvelle Hell'. I strongly agree. Nibble and nosh as you toss. Your tastebuds are, ultimately, your best guide.

PREPARING AND STORING SALAD GREENS

Firm lettuces are easily cleaned by cutting out the stem. Sever it about 25 cm/1 in deep into the head, and hold the lettuce under running cold water. Then turn the head right-side up on a colander placed in the sink. Remove the outside wilted leaves, pull the head apart, pat the leaves dry with a clean teatowel or kitchen paper towel, and put the lettuce in the refrigerator to crisp. Cos, escarole, and other clusters of firm lettuce leaves may be pulled apart first, then washed, patted dry, and crisped in the refrigerator. Use a little more care with round and other soft lettuces. Float the leaves in cold water and spread them out on kitchen paper towels to air-dry.

Remove large, gritty, tough stalks from spinach by folding the leaves in half lengthways so that the sides touch, then pull the stalks down along the leaves.

To store greens, line a perforated, thick, plastic bag with slightly damp kitchen paper towels, insert the greens and refrigerate. Chill your salad plates, too, if you want to really show off your icy greens. If you want to hurry things up, or you have difficulty keeping greens fresh for several days, try some of the already washed and bagged greens in the supermarkets. They are more expensive, but at least you won't end up discarding them. Some come with packets of dressings, too, but they are usually full of preservatives and calories, and you will probably want to replace them with your own homemade varieties.

COMBINING SALAD GREENS

In general, the darker the green, the stronger the flavour. If you are using a mild-flavoured lettuce, such as iceberg, you may want to add peppery notes by combining it with watercress, rocket, young dandelion, or nasturtium blossoms. Conversely, you would probably not want to mix a salad with too many

PREPARING AND STORING HERBS

Rinse herbs in cold water and remove discoloured leaves before using. Fresh herbs are bursting with flavour and only a single strong pungent herb is used in many salads so that one flavour doesn't cancel out another. To keep herbs from turning an unsightly brown, place them in an airtight glass jar or plastic container and refrigerate. If your herbs have their stalks attached, such as parsley or coriander, store in the refrigerator in a lidded glass or in a jar with water covering the roots.

You can freeze any leftover small bunches of green herbs, such as mint or chives, by washing and drying them, wrapping them in foil or plastic, and placing them in the freezer where they will stay flavourful for about two months. Use these frozen herbs for cooking only, though, because while freezing doesn't ruin the flavour, it does make them look limp.

Dried herbs are used directly from their containers. They are stronger than fresh herbs, so substitute a teaspoon of dried herb for a tablespoon of fresh. Store dried herbs away from heat in a cool, dimly lit place. They will keep for up to a year.

DRYING HERBS

You can successfully dry your own herbs by tying stalks together in small bunches and hanging them upside down and out of direct sunlight in a cupboard, attic or kitchen. When herbs are dry, in about two weeks' time, place them on a kitchen paper towel and rub the stalks between your palms until all the leaves have fallen off.

For thyme, rosemary and oregano, you can strip the leaves from the stalk by simply running your thumb and index finger down the stalk. Discard the stalks and then rub leaves through a fine-mesh strainer to remove any small bits of stray stalk. Store your dried leaves in a glass jar with a tight-fitting lid, and label the jars carefully.

OILS AND VINEGARS

Oils and vinegars are the basic ingredients that liven up salad greens. Combining two parts of oil and one part vinegar, then adding a little sugar, salt or pepper to taste, makes a tasty coating for greens. Adjust the ratio of oil and vinegar according to the acidity of the vinegar you use, the type of oil, and your own tastebuds. If you like tomato in your salads, but are subject to heartburn, it is wise to place the tomatoes on top of the salad after tossing. Tomatoes have a lot of acid, and there is even more acid in vinegar. Japanese rice vinegar is less acidic, so you may want to use it instead of the more standard vinegars.

If you are concerned about cholesterol – and oils are loaded with fats, some good and some bad – try using less than a half-and-half ratio, or substitute a little extracted fresh vegetable juice for some of the oil in a recipe. If you like creamy dressings, but want to avoid dairy fat, add about 15 ml/1 tbsp each of milk and Dijon mustard to a 225 ml/8 fl oz carton of plain low-fat or non-fat yogurt, then season the mixture with a teaspoon of dried herbs, or one or two teaspoons of fresh herbs, and a dab of honey.

Oils and vinegars can be stored in attractive bottles to display in the kitchen or pantry. Imagine how pretty they will be if stored in beautiful Spanish green glass bottles, glass Granada-style bottles, or any pretty wine bottles you have saved. A fish-shaped wine bottle and round-sided, clear, slivovitz bottle are my favourites. Just remember to tightly cork or seal the bottles.

OILS FOR SALADS

Do not store any oils near the cooker, or any other warm area, because heat can cause deterioration. Refrigeration, on the other hand, can make oils turn milky-looking and cause them to congeal. Simply place them on a shelf in a cupboard or on display but out of sunlight. Most oils generally have plenty of vitamin E in them, a substance that keeps them from turning rancid quickly, but polyunsaturated oils turn rancid rapidly unless treated with preservatives and should be refrigerated. Olive oil keeps for about a year in the refrigerator, but it will congeal and turn cloudy, so return it to room temperature before using. It can be stored on the shelf for up to six months. Delicate oils, such as walnut or infused olive oils, should be refrigerated and used rapidly.

INFUSED OILS

These are oils that have herbs steeped or soaked in them. They have long been used in Mediterranean, Indian, Chinese and other oriental cooking. It is best to buy infused oils that have been commercially prepared because preparing infused oils at home, especially those oils containing garlic and onion, can promote the growth of botulism. Commercially prepared and with the proper preservatives, however, these oils can be considered perfectly safe and are delicious. They should be refrigerated after opening.

A store-bought infused oil can liven up a vinaigrette. Or you can dip dense bread into flavoured oil for an imaginative alternative to butter. Flavoured oil can also provide the perfect complement to pasta, pizza or bruschetta. Infused oil can top a baked potato or substitute for butter and milk to make garlicky mashed potatoes. You could also try sautéeing fresh artichoke hearts in an infused oil, or drizzling a little over poached salmon, grilled aubergine, roasted pepper or other vegetables. A low-fat or non-fat prepared mayonnaise can also be jazzed up with a little infused oil.

GLOSSARY OF SALAD OILS

CANOLA OR RAPESEED OIL
This oil contains one-twelfth of the saturated fat contained in tropical oils, such as coconut oil.

CORN OIL
This oil is also low in saturated fat. Although it tastes rather bland, it can be used for frying and baking, as well as in salad dressings.

HAZELNUT OIL
Extracted from hazelnuts, this oil is very aromatic. It can be combined with a less strongly flavoured oil for a rich, nutty-tasting salad dressing. Heat destroys its flavour.

OLIVE OIL
A staple in the Mediterranean diet, olive oil is healthy, as well as tasty. It is the best oil to use in a simple dressing such as a vinaigrette or as a velvety 'thickener' in many other delicious dressings.

PEANUT OIL
Extracted from peanuts, this oil is often used in Asian dishes, but can also be used in many salad dressings. It is slightly higher in saturated fat than rapeseed and corn oil.

SAFFLOWER OIL
This delicate, relatively tasteless oil is low in saturated fat.

SESAME OIL
Extracted from sesame seeds, this oil is used in Chinese cooking. Like peanut oil, it is slightly higher in saturated fat than rapeseed and corn oil, but not as fatty as tropical oils.

TROPICAL OILS
These oils – such as coconut, palm or palm kernel – are highly saturated and should be avoided, if possible.

WALNUT OIL
Extracted from walnuts, this oil is used in well-known salads, such as the Waldorf. It has a rich flavour, which is destroyed by heating it, and should be used sparingly.

VINEGARS AND OTHER ACIDIC FLAVOURINGS

VINEGAR, A MAJOR food preservative and pickler, is as old as civilization itself. In 400 B.C., Hippocrates used it to treat patients, and people still use it today for everything from headaches to removing lime deposits on fine crystal. Vinegar contains essential amino acids, vitamins, minerals and enzymes. It is receptive to added flavours and keeps indefinitely in a cool, dark place. Furthermore, it is perfectly safe to make and keep preserved vinegars at home.

Most herbs can be used to flavour vinegars: tarragon, rosemary, thyme, marjoram, parsley, basil, fennel, dill and sage. They can be used individually or in combinations. It is best to use fresh herbs; if you pick them yourself, make sure to select sprigs without any flowers. Bruising the herbs slightly will help to release their flavour. Try placing a little fresh oregano and small fresh chillies in a clean, dry bottle filled with white or red wine vinegar. Leave the vinegar for two to three weeks to infuse; try to make a point of shaking it every day. Strain the vinegar, pressing down well on the herbs. Taste to see if the herb flavour is strong enough. If it is not, repeat the process. Then use the finished vinegar to make a spicy salad dressing. Experiment with other fresh herbs, and store your creations in pretty bottles. You will have made a vinegar for pennies that specialist food shops sell at prices approaching good table wine.

It is also possible to flavour vinegar with fruit for a fresh dressing for rich meats such as duck or game and a perfect complement to salads containing fruit. Try a raspberry vinegar mixed with walnut oil, mustard, salt and pepper for an unforgettable vinaigrette.

Because vinegar and vinaigrettes have such powerful flavourings, it is important to consider when to serve them. The French have the right idea on salads containing vinegar. They serve them after the main course so that the vinegar does not interfere with the wine. Americans prefer their salads with vinaigrettes at the start of a meal. If you are watching your weight, you might want to consider eating a large salad of mixed greens and raw vegetables sprinkled with a vinaigrette. Vinegar is known to suppress the appetite in some people, and it might enable you to cut down on your main course and dessert portions.

There are many vinegars readily available today from supermarkets and specialist food shops. Balsamic vinegar is a

barrel-aged vinegar, dark in colour with a mellow sweet-sour character. It is made from the Trebbiano grape in the region surrounding Modena, Italy, and aged in wooden casks for between two and forty years. Drizzle some on fish for a change from lemon, or use in marinades and dressings.

GLOSSARY OF SALAD VINEGARS

CHAMPAGNE VINEGAR
This vinegar is flavored with champagne.

CIDER VINEGAR
Made from the juice of apples, cider vinegar has a fruity flavour that works well in salads. It is also used for pickling and preserving.

DISTILLED WHITE VINEGAR
Made from grain alcohol, this vinegar is used mostly in pickling. It has a harsh flavour.

MALT VINEGAR
Made from barley, this vinegar is mostly used for pickling but can also be used in salad dressings.

RASPBERRY VINEGAR
Made from raspberries and vinegar, this vinegar has a fruity flavour that is good in fruit salads.

RICE WINE VINEGAR
Made from sake, this vinegar has a natural sweetness and is used predominantly in Chinese and Japanese cooking.

SHERRY VINEGAR
Made from Spanish sherry, this vinegar is matured and has a subtle sweetness from the brandy that is used in sherry-making. It makes a wonderful ingredient in salad dressings.

WINE VINEGARS
Either red or white, these vinegars are excellent in dressings and are very versatile. White wine vinegar is a good choice for an infused vinegar.

GLOSSARY OF SALAD GREENS

ARUGULA OR ROCKET

This green herb is also called roquette, rucola and ruchetta. It has a soft texture and peppery, sharp taste. Many cooks believe it is best used alone in salads, served with only a simple dressing.

BASIL

This sweet, perfumey 'royal herb' of ancient Greece is a member of the mint family and has a flavour like liquorice and cloves. It is a staple in Mediterranean cooking. Fresh basil makes a beautiful garnish, but you can also buy it dried.

BIBB

Before the new designer greens became popular, yellowy green Bibb, grown in limestone soil, was the most sought-after lettuce. It has a tender texture and sharp flavour, which goes well with rich dressings and ingredients, such as crab. It is also good when mixed with other greens.

BOK CHOY OR CHINESE LEAVES

Sometimes called *pak choi*, or Chinese cabbage, chard, or white mustard cabbage, this elongated cabbage unfurls dark green leaves from long white stalks. *Choi* can be translated as both cabbage and the generic term for vegetable, and the green is beloved by the Chinese. Choose heads with smooth white stalks and crisp, unblemished leaves. It will keep for about four days if stored in a plastic bag in the refrigerator.

BOSTON

This lettuce is also called butter, Simpson, and, incorrectly, Bibb. It is a round, loosely packed head with tender, soft leaves and a mild flavour.

BRONZE

Also called red lettuce, this garden lettuce has bronze-edged leaves and is similar in texture and taste to leaf (or garden) lettuce.

BUTTERHEAD

The butterheads are the most popular lettuce group. Often called round lettuce, the leaves are soft and smooth-edged. Most are summer varieties but a few are hardy, while others are grown in greenhouses.

CABBAGE

A firmly packed head of thick, heavy, pale green or purple-red leaves. Discard the tough outer leaves before using. Cabbage is usually shredded and used in coleslaw or mixed with salad greens.

CHERVIL

A fern-like plant with feathery anise-flavored leaves, chervil is used in salads and cold dishes. It is one of the classic ingredients in *fines herbes*.

ENDIVE

Called frisée by the French, and chicory in the United States, this green has feathery but sturdy leaves that spread out. Endive is yellow at the centre, and becomes a pale to darker green outside. Its crisp texture and slightly bitter taste add pizzazz to a mix of other, more delicately flavoured, greens.

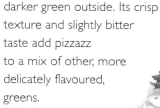

CHIVES

This long, thin onion grass has a pleasing, subtle, mild flavour that seems to spread over the palate. The blossoms can also be eaten.

CORIANDER

Also known as cilantro or Chinese parsley, this herb has a pungent mintiness and is related to the parsley family. Some think it tastes like citrus zest, while others find its flavour soapy, so use the herb judiciously if company is expected. It is used in the cuisines of Mexico, the Orient, the Caribbean and India.

LAMB'S LETTUCE

Also called mâche and corn salad, this delicate but full-flavoured lettuce has downy, medium-to-dark, blue-green, spoon-shaped leaves and a sweet, nutty flavour. It is excellent when dressed with a classic vinaigrette.

DANDELION

Long considered an ugly, invasive weed, dandelion leaves are cultivated in France, and dandelion-growers are beginning to appear in the United States. The tart flavour of the narrow, spiky, dark green leaves seems to be appealing to more and more people.

DILL

This herb has a light caraway flavour and feathery, fern-like green leaves. Traditionally, it is used in making pickles, for flavouring Indian yogurt dishes and in gravlax, but it is now being used in salads, too. The herb makes a lovely garnish, especially for fish dishes.

CHICORY

This salad vegetable grows on a firm, narrow, pale yellow head and has tightly packed, long, pointed, waxy leaves and a tangy flavour. Its leaves can transform a salad into a still-life masterpiece.

ESCAROLE

Also known as batavian endive, batavia, or chicory escarole, this somewhat bitter lettuce has a flat spread-out head with a yellow centre. The dark green leaves are curly, firm, and robust in texture.

LAMB'S TONGUE

This lettuce has very small spears on delicate stalks and a mild flavour.

ICEBERG

A round, firm lettuce, this longtime favourite keeps well and is crispy, but it is watery and not very flavourful. It does, however, deliver the requisite crunch that many people demand in a salad or a sandwich.

LEAF LETTUCE

Also called garden lettuce, there are several varieties of this pleasant, mild-tasting lettuce with soft, long, crumpled-edged leaves. It is often used to prettify a delicate salad or to embellish and add crunch to sandwiches.

MESCLUN

This term, popular on restaurant menus, simply means 'mixture' in French. It is usually a combination of lettuces, endive, rocket or watercress, and other herb greens. Because some of the leaves are smaller than more standard lettuce leaves, such as iceberg, mesclun is sometimes called 'baby greens'.

MINT

This herb is available in many varieties, including apple mint, spearmint and peppermint. It makes a lovely decoration and flavour enhancer for desserts and fruit salads.

MISTICANZA

Like the French word 'mesclun', this is simply a mixture of lettuces.

MUSTARD GREENS

These bright, light green leaves have scalloped edges and a soft texture. They have a pungent mustard flavour that is delicious with robust foods, such as beef.

NASTURTIUM

The flower heads of nasturtium add a peppery taste and gorgeous colour to a green or mixed salad. Use only fresh, unsprayed blossoms.

OAK LEAF

Also called salad bowl, red oak leaf and lolla rossa, this tangy lettuce is available in both red and green colours. Its velvety leaves are paddle-shaped, like oak leaves, and it makes a pretty addition to any salad.

PARSLEY

Varieties include the familiar curly-leaf and the increasingly popular Italian flat-leaf. The herb looks pretty, tastes clean, and refreshes the breath. It is also rich in vitamins. Use the fresh herb; dried parsley is tasteless.

PINE NUTS

These are actually the kernels of the pine-tree seed. They are tender and cream-coloured with a slightly oily, delicate flavour. Pine nuts were a native staple crop of the Pueblo Indians. They are often toasted when used in salads.

RADICCHIO

Also called red chicory, this crisp, trendy, slightly bitter lettuce is as Italian as its name. Its small leaves are a colourful addition to other greens in a mixed salad and can also be used as a capacious 'cup' for salads, particularly seafood salads.

ROMAINE OR COS

Also called Kos (the name comes from the Greek island of Kos), this lettuce has an elongated, cylindrical head and long, stiff, thick-veined leaves, which are usually medium-dark to dark green on the outside and greenish-white or pale yellow near the centre. Unlike most lettuces, the lighter-coloured leaves have the stronger flavour. It is pungent and hardy, full of vitamins and minerals, and good with assertive dishes, such as Caesar salad.

SPRING ONIONS

Spring onions have long, thin stalks with white bulbs and green tops. They can often be substituted for chives.

SHALLOTS

This member of the onion family, originating in the Middle East, has a small, round, pinkish-white bulb and golden brown skin. It has a subtle, complex flavour that is somewhere between onions and garlic. The great chefs adore shallots, which are now being used in elegant oriental dishes, as well as in French cuisine.

SPINACH

This herb was first grown in Persia and the Middle East. It has dark green leaves, some crinkly, on stalks. After lettuce, spinach is the most popular green leaf in North America, although most of it is consumed in cooked form. Some find raw spinach hard to digest, so use it judiciously in salads prepared for guests.

TARRAGON

This is a tall plant that tastes like peppery anise. It is used in classic French cooking and makes a great flavouring for vinegar.

TURNIP GREENS

These can resemble napped radish leaves and have a sharp taste. Remove large stalks by folding leaves in half lengthways, then pull the stalks down along the leaves. The bulb can be grated and eaten raw.

WATERCRESS

This green grows on small stalks and has many small, round, dark green petals. Watercress is sold banded in bunches and has a distinct, lively, pleasant taste.

Dressings, Vinegars & Vinaigrettes

INGREDIENTS FOR SALAD DRESSINGS

EGGS

Some eggs have been shown to contain salmonella so the elderly, young, babies, pregnant women and people with poor immune defence systems are advised not to eat raw or lightly cooked eggs.

GARLIC

Garlic is nearly always used raw in dressings and marinades, so it really is important that firm cloves that are as fresh as possible are used. Ideally, the cloves should not have green sprouts growing out of their tops, but if they do, be sure to remove all of the sprout as it tastes bitter.

Buy garlic that feels firm, is shiny with the paper skin still attached, not peeling off in flakes. Store garlic in a cool, dark, airy place.

The intensity of the garlic flavour varies according to how the cloves are prepared. For salad dressings, it is best to crush the cloves with a small pinch of salt because not only does chopping give a harsher flavour than crushing them, but many people do not like to bite on small pieces of raw garlic. Another way to add a mild garlic flavour to a salad dressing is to roast the cloves. To give a mild garlic flavour to a salad, the salad bowl can be rubbed with a cut clove of garlic.

HERBS

Most of the recipes in this book have been made using fresh herbs, except where dried ones are mentioned. With the exception of spice rubs, I never use dried herbs. If I do not have the fresh herb that I want already growing in my garden, either in the ground or in a pot, in a window box or in a pot on the windowsill (a surprising number of herbs can be grown successfully in tubs, window boxes and pots on windowsills) and I am unable to buy fresh herbs, I buy frozen or freeze-dried herbs, which most supermarkets now stock. Many supermarkets and greengrocers also sell herbs growing in pots.

Store fresh herbs in 'stay-fresh' bags in the refrigerator.

Fresh herbs can vary quite considerably in flavour, so it is important to taste each batch you are using and to adjust the amount you use as necessary.

OILS

Oils are the foundation of most salad dressings and are an important addition to marinades because they add flavour to the food being marinated, lubricate it and keep it moist during cooking.

PEPPER

Along with salt, pepper (usually black) is the common seasoning for salad dressings. White pepper may be used where dark specks of black pepper would spoil the appearance of a recipe.

To give your salad dressings the best flavour use freshly ground peppercorns rather than ground pepper as this is too fine and powdery and lacks the fresh piquancy of freshly ground corns.

SALT

Many experienced cooks prefer to use sea salt or other coarse salts, believing their flavour to be superior to ordinary table salt, but at a recent tasting of a wide selection of different salts, involving top British food writers and chefs, the salt that came out on top was common table salt!

SOY SAUCE

Now used not only in Chinese and Japanese cooking, but also in other recipes to add depth to the flavour, as well as a characteristic taste.

LIGHT SOY SAUCE

This is light in colour but it has a full flavour and is more salty than dark soy sauce. In Chinese food shops light soy sauce is known as Superior Soy. It is the sauce that is generally used for cooking; the word 'light' may not always be included.

DARK SOY SAUCE

This is matured for longer than light soy sauce so has a darker color. Its flavor is slightly stronger than light soy sauce and it is slightly thicker. It is known as Soy Superior Sauce in Chinese food shops, and is the one most often sold there. Its most common use is in dipping sauces.

SPICES

For the best flavour, use freshly ground spices rather than ready ground ones. To get the maximum flavour from the whole spices, before grinding them, heat them gently in a heated heavy frying pan until they smell fragrant.

Because the flavour of spices deteriorates with age, buy spices in small amounts that you will use quickly; if you have any for more than six months, throw them away. Keep the spices in a cool, dark, dry place.

SZECHUAN PEPPERCORNS

Reddish brown colour and a sharp, mildly spicy flavour that has a hint of lavender. Szechuan peppercorns do not come from the same family as white, black and green peppercorns and do not have the same 'hotness'. Szechuan peppercorns are usually dry roasted and ground before using to bring out their full flavour.

VINEGAR

Vinegar is the second most important ingredient in salad dressings and marinades, after oil. It is important in both dressings and marinades for adding flavour and piquancy, and in dressings it is vital for forming an emulsion with the oil, so thickening the sauce, while in marinades it tenderizes meat, poultry, game and fish.

FLORIDA VINAIGRETTE

Makes about 450 ml/¾ pint

In Florida, the juice of freshly squeezed Key limes would be used for this tart vinaigrette, but even when made with bottled citrus juice, this dressing still tastes great. Drizzle the vinaigrette over salad greens, or douse over poached and chilled seafood, such as prawns or scallops: it also adds pizzazz to roasted potatoes and steamed vegetables.

INGREDIENTS

225 ml/8 fl oz fresh or bottled lime or lemon juice

25 g/1 oz onion, finely chopped

1 red pepper, cored, seeded and finely chopped

1 tbsp finely chopped ginger root

1 tbsp crushed garlic

2 tbsp finely chopped fresh dill

1 tbsp Dijon mustard

5 ml/1 tsp rice wine vinegar

100 ml/4 fl oz light olive oil or 100 ml/4 fl oz of the juice extracted from red peppers with 10 ml/2 tsp olive oil added

salt and freshly ground pepper

WHISK TOGETHER THE lime or lemon juice, onion, pepper, ginger, garlic, dill, mustard, vinegar and olive oil or red pepper juice in a nonreactive medium bowl until well combined. Season with salt and pepper to taste.

CONTINENTAL HERB DRESSING

Makes about 225 ml/8 fl oz

You can almost see spring making its long-awaited debut after a cold winter in this aromatic dressing, which incorporates several favourite herbs. It is delicious served over any mixture of greens, particularly French Mesclun.

INGREDIENTS

100 ml/4 fl oz vegetable oil

50 ml/2 fl oz vinegar

¼ tsp salt

pinch of cayenne pepper

1 tbsp finely chopped fresh parsley

1 tbsp finely chopped fresh basil

1 tbsp finely chopped fresh chervil

1 tbsp finely chopped fresh oregano

freshly ground black pepper

WHISK TOGETHER THE vegetable oil, vinegar, salt, cayenne pepper and herbs in a medium bowl. Add pepper to taste and chill in the refrigerator for 2–24 hours.

Florida Vinaigrette ▶

CLASSIC FRENCH VINAIGRETTE

Makes about 225 ml/8 fl oz

In the United States, this vinaigrette was the first recipe listed under salad dressings in the
1896 *Boston Cooking-School Cook Book*, one of the first definitive cookbooks published in the country.
This recipe includes prepared mustard, a fairly modern addition to the blend.

INGREDIENTS

½ tsp salt

⅛ tsp freshly ground pepper

50 ml/2 fl oz vinegar or lemon juice

¼–½ tsp Dijon mustard

175 ml/6 fl oz walnut or olive oil

WHISK TOGETHER THE salt, pepper, vinegar or lemon juice, mustard and walnut or olive oil in a nonreactive medium bowl until well combined. The dressing will keep for about 3 days in the refrigerator.

EMIGRÉ'S COOKED FRENCH DRESSING

Makes about 225 ml/8 fl oz

A nobleman who emigrated from France, Chevalier d'Albignac, is said to have introduced salads of raw greens dressed in vinaigrettes to England in the late 1700s. While his recipes have been lost to history, they were reportedly just as complex as this one, which I have named after him. It tastes great over any mixture of salad greens.

INGREDIENTS

½ tbsp salt

½ tbsp dry mustard

1¼ tbsp sugar

1 egg, lightly beaten

37.5 ml/2½ tbsp melted unsalted butter

175 ml/6 fl oz cream

pinch of cayenne pepper

50 ml/2 fl oz white wine vinegar

MIX SALT, MUSTARD, sugar, egg, melted butter, cream and cayenne pepper together in a nonreactive bowl. Add vinegar 5 ml/ 1 tsp at a time, whisking constantly. Transfer to a double saucepan and cook over boiling water, stirring constantly until the mixture thickens. Leave to cool and serve.

The ingredients for Classic French Vinaigrette ▶

TRY MY THAI DRESSING

Makes about 225 ml/8 fl oz

This Thai-inspired dressing is especially good with steamed or grilled aubergine, which has been cooled to room temperature. It is also delicious when served over salad greens that have some julienned strips of red cabbage mixed in for colour and texture.

INGREDIENTS

2 shallots, finely chopped

2 garlic cloves, finely chopped

2 tbsp finely chopped fresh coriander

1/2–1 tsp crushed dried red pepper flakes

50 ml/2 fl oz Thai *nam pla* fish sauce or Vietnamese *nuoc nam* fish sauce

175 ml/6 fl oz fresh lemon or lime juice

1 tsp finely grated lemon or lime rind

3 spring onions, finely chopped

PLACE THE SHALLOTS, garlic, coriander, red pepper flakes, fish sauce, lemon or lime juice, lemon or lime rind and spring onions in a nonreactive bowl and mix well to combine. Set aside at room temperature for about 15 minutes to let the flavours blend, then serve.

NUTTY ORIENTAL DRESSING

Makes about 300 ml/1/2 pint

Inspired by Vietnamese cooking, this tasty dressing is great on lamb and other hot or cold meats, as well as on salad greens. If you like assertive flavours, you can also pour a little over rice noodles. You can find *nuoc nam* fish sauce in oriental food shops.

INGREDIENTS

22.5 ml/1 1/2 tbsp peanut, sesame or rapeseed oil

1 garlic clove, chopped

15 ml/1 tbsp oyster sauce

15 ml/1 tbsp *nuoc nam* fish sauce or Thai *nam pla* fish sauce

pinch of sugar

1 tbsp finely chopped fresh or canned chilli

5 tbsp fresh mint leaves, sliced if large

5 tbsp crushed dry-roasted peanuts

WARM THE OIL in a wok, but do not let it sizzle. Add the garlic, oyster sauce, fish sauce, sugar, and chilli, stirring constantly. Stir in the mint, remove from the heat, and let cool to room temperature. Add the peanuts and serve immediately.

◀ *Try My Thai Dressing*
with steamed aubergine

DILL DRESSING

Makes about 450 ml/¾ pint

This is a perfect dressing for a cucumber salad, but it also makes a great dip for crudités, or serve it with fish for a refreshing change from tartare sauce. It can also be used instead of plain mayonnaise to make devilled eggs.

INGREDIENTS

225 ml/8 fl oz plain non-fat or low-fat yogurt

225 ml/8 fl oz non-fat or low-fat mayonnaise

1 tbsp chopped spring onions

1½ tbsp finely chopped fresh dill

10 ml/2 tsp lemon juice

freshly ground black pepper

PLACE THE YOGURT, mayonnaise, spring onions, dill and lemon juice in a medium bowl and mix together well to combine. Season with pepper to taste. Cover and chill in the refrigerator for 2–24 hours. Serve chilled.

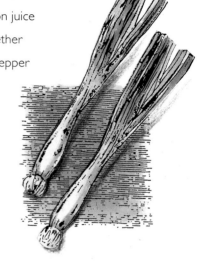

RUSSIAN DOLL DRESSING

Makes about 350 ml/12 fl oz

If you like caviar, you will love this Russian dressing. Use it to toss with salad greens or potatoes, or spoon it over a combination of diced potatoes and beetroot. It makes an elegant topping for potato pancakes.

INGREDIENTS

225 ml/8 fl oz light or non-fat mayonnaise

1 tbsp prepared horseradish or grated fresh horseradish

3 tbsp chilled caviar or salmon roe

5 ml/1 tsp Worcestershire sauce

1.25 ml/¼ tsp hot pepper sauce

1 tsp grated onion

PLACE THE MAYONNAISE, horseradish, caviar or salmon roe, Worcestershire sauce, hot pepper sauce and onion in a small bowl and mix well to combine. Serve immediately.

LOW-FAT BLUE CHEESE DRESSING

Makes about 350–450 ml/12–15 fl oz

This dressing is delicious served over salad greens. Although it tastes creamy and rich, it is low in fat because yogurt and buttermilk replace the traditional oil or mayonnaise.

INGREDIENTS

225 ml/8 fl oz plain non-fat or low-fat yogurt

100 g/4 oz blue cheese, crumbled

100 ml/4 fl oz buttermilk

15 g/½ oz fresh parsley, finely chopped

15 ml/1 tbsp light olive oil

5 ml/1 tsp dry sherry or cider vinegar

freshly ground black pepper

PLACE THE YOGURT, cheese, buttermilk, parsley, olive oil and sherry or vinegar in a small bowl and mix together to combine. Season with pepper to taste. Cover and chill for 2–24 hours before using. The dressing will keep for about 3 days in the refrigerator.

ORANGE-POPPY SEED DRESSING

Makes about 100 ml/4 fl oz

This dressing originates from Pennsylvania country and various farming regions of the Midwest of the United States. It combines well with fruit and avocado salads.

INGREDIENTS

100 ml/4 fl oz plain or vanilla low-fat yogurt

7.5 ml/½ tbsp honey

½ tsp dry mustard

1 tbsp grated onion

7.5 ml/½ tbsp frozen orange juice concentrate, thawed

½ tsp poppy seeds

2 drops hot pepper sauce (optional)

½ tsp finely grated orange or lemon rind

IN A MEDIUM bowl, place the yogurt, honey, dry mustard, onion, orange juice concentrate, poppy seeds, hot pepper sauce and orange or lemon rind and stir well to combine. Cover and chill in the refrigerator for 2–24 hours. The dressing will keep for about 3 days in the refrigerator.

SUN-DRIED TOMATO DRESSING

Makes about 350 ml/12 fl oz

This naturally sweet dressing is excellent when served on strong-flavoured salad greens, such
as rocket, or on pasta, bruschetta or small pizza rounds that have been garnished with torn leaves of salad greens.
Use a high-quality brand of extra virgin olive oil for the finest flavour.

INGREDIENTS

12 sun-dried tomatoes, soaked in
water until plump, then drained

2 garlic cloves

1 tsp dried oregano

1 tbsp tomato purée

90 ml/6 tbsp balsamic vinegar

salt and freshly ground black pepper

100 ml/4 fl oz olive oil

PLACE THE TOMATOES, garlic, oregano, tomato purée, and vinegar in a food processor or blender and purée. Add salt and pepper to taste. With the machine running, gradually add the oil in a steady stream until well combined. The dressing will keep for about 3 days in the refrigerator.

RHINELAND DRESSING

Makes about 175 ml/6 fl oz

This is a classic German dressing for vegetables, meat or fish.
With its heady addition of brandy, it can really jazz up leftovers.

INGREDIENTS

30 ml/2 tbsp olive oil

50 ml/2 fl oz cider vinegar

50 ml/2 fl oz brandy

salt and freshly ground black pepper

WHISK THE OLIVE oil, cider vinegar and brandy in a small bowl, mixing well to combine. Season with salt and pepper to taste, and serve immediately.

*Sun-dried Tomato Dressing spread on
crostini* ▶

THOUSAND ISLAND DRESSING

Makes about 350 ml/12 fl oz

The islands to which the title refers are in the St Lawrence Seaway on the Canadian border. The original nineteenth-century dressing did not contain mayonnaise but was simply a vinaigrette dressing flavoured and coloured pink by paprika pepper or tomato purée. Serve with crisp green salads, egg, potato or prawn salads.

INGREDIENTS

225 ml/8 fl oz mayonnaise

2 tbsp stuffed olives, finely chopped

1 tbsp finely chopped green pepper

1 tbsp finely chopped onion or chives

1 tbsp chopped fresh parsley

1 hard-boiled egg, finely chopped

few drops of hot pepper sauce

salt and freshly ground black pepper

PUT THE MAYONNAISE into a bowl. Stir in the remaining ingredients.

SAUCE VIERGE
(TOMATO AND OLIVE OIL DRESSING)

Makes about 350 ml/12 fl oz

For this dressing you really should have well-flavoured, sun-ripened tomatoes and good quality olive oil. When the sauce is left to infuse for 30 minutes there is no need for the saucepan to be over heat. The dressing goes well with all types of salads and can also be served with grilled fish or cold chicken, turkey and fish.

INGREDIENTS

4 well-flavoured tomatoes, peeled and seeded

2 small garlic cloves, unpeeled

200 ml/7 fl oz virgin olive oil

2 tbsp chopped fresh basil or chervil

2 tbsp chopped parsley

1 tbsp chopped tarragon or thyme

8 coriander seeds, roasted and crushed

salt and freshly ground black pepper

CUT THE TOMATOES into 5 mm/ ¼-in dice and put into a bowl. Stir in the remaining ingredients.

Put the bowl over a saucepan of hot water, cover and leave for 30 minutes. Remove from the pan and leave until cold.

◀ Thousand Island Dressing

GARLIC VINEGAR

Makes about 750 ml/1¼ pints

Deliciously fragranced with the scent of garlic, this vinegar is useful for salad and pasta dishes. If you wish to give a bottle as a gift, thread 2–3 garlic cloves per bottle on to a wooden cocktail stick and add to the vinegar.

INGREDIENTS

12 plump garlic cloves

750 ml/1¼ pints white wine vinegar

LIGHTLY CRUSH THE garlic cloves and put them into a jar or bottle. Pour in the vinegar, cover and shake the jar or bottle. Leave in a cool, dark place for 2–3 weeks.

If the flavour of the vinegar is strong enough, strain it and re-bottle.

VINEGAR FLAVORED WITH HERBES DE PROVENCE

Makes about 750 ml/1¼ pints

Bring back memories of summer holidays with this aromatic vinegar.
A fresh herb sprig can be added to the prepared vinegar, if desired.

INGREDIENTS

3 large sprigs of tarragon

3 large sprigs of thyme

3 sprigs of rosemary

4 bay leaves

pinch of fennel seeds

750 ml/1¼ pints white wine vinegar

LIGHTLY BRUISE THE herbs and then pack them into a jar or bottle. Pour in the vinegar and close the bottle tightly. Shake the jar or bottle and leave in a cool, dark place for 2–3 weeks, shaking the jar or bottle daily.

Strain the vinegar, pressing down well on the herbs. Taste it to see if the herb flavour is strong enough. If it is not, repeat the process.

FRUIT VINEGAR

Makes about 450 ml/16 fl oz

Use this fruity vinegar to add flavour to summer dressings and marinades.
Add a few whole berries to the vinegar to decorate, if liked.

INGREDIENTS

450 g/1lb fruit, such as raspberries,
strawberries or blackcurrants

450 ml/16 fl oz white wine vinegar

50 g/2 oz sugar

PUT THE FRUIT into a nonreactive bowl or jar. Add a little of the vinegar and crush the fruit with the back of a wooden spoon to release the juice. Add the remaining vinegar, cover and leave in a cool place for 1 week, stirring occasionally.

Strain the vinegar into a saucepan, add the sugar and heat gently, stirring until the sugar has dissolved. Bring to the boil. Cool.

Pour the vinegar into a clean bottle, cover and store in a dark, cool place.

ORANGE VINEGAR

Makes about 1 l/1¾ pints

A tangy-tasting vinegar that goes particularly well with rich meat and poultry dishes.
Try varying the recipe with fresh lemons or limes to give a different taste.

INGREDIENTS

3 large oranges

1 l/1¾ pints white wine vinegar

1 small orange, for garnish

PARE THE RIND from the 3 large oranges, taking care not to include any white pith. Put the rind into a clean large jar. Cut the oranges in half and squeeze out the juice. Pour into the jar, seal and shake. Leave in a cool, dark place for 3 weeks, shaking the jar occasionally.

Strain the vinegar and re-bottle. Thinly pare some of the rind from the small orange so no pith is included. Cut the rind into thin strips and add 3 strips to each bottle.

TUNA MAYONNAISE

Makes about 350 ml/12 fl oz

Tuna mayonnaise is the classic sauce to spoon over the Italian dish of poached veal, *Vitello Tonnato*, but it is
so delicious that it has many other uses. For example, it perks up potato, tomato, red pepper, courgette, plain, crisp
green, fish and shellfish salads, and goes well with hard-boiled eggs and avocados. For extra zest and depth of flavour,
add some chopped capers and anchovy fillets; tarragon vinegar can be used instead of lemon juice.

INGREDIENTS

1 small garlic clove

100 g/3½ oz canned tuna, drained

about 30 ml/2 tbsp lemon juice

leaves from a sprig of parsley

1 egg or 2 egg yolks (see page 18)

1½ tsp Dijon mustard

225 ml/8 fl oz olive oil

115 ml/4 fl oz sunflower oil

salt and freshly ground black pepper

PUT THE GARLIC, tuna, lemon juice,
parsley, egg and mustard into a
blender. Mix together briefly to make a
smooth paste. With the motor
running, slowly pour in the olive oil
then the sunflower oil until well
emulsified and thick.

Season to taste and add more
lemon juice, if liked.

BOILED SALAD DRESSING

Makes about 1½ cups

This old-fashioned dressing is useful for those who do not like oil. It goes well with
shredded celeriac and cabbage, green and vegetable salads, and eggs.

INGREDIENTS

20 g/¾ oz plain flour

1 tsp dry mustard powder

15 g/½ oz sugar

pinch of cayenne pepper

2 egg yolks

175 ml/6 fl oz milk

30 ml/2 tbsp melted butter

60 ml/4 tbsp white wine vinegar

salt and freshly ground black pepper

MIX THE FLOUR, mustard powder,
sugar and cayenne pepper
together in a saucepan. Stir in the milk,
egg yolks, butter and vinegar until
evenly mixed then heat very gently,
whisking constantly, until thickened.

Season with salt and pepper to
taste and leave to cool, stirring
occasionally to prevent a skin forming.

*Tuna Mayonnaise with chargrilled red
peppers* ▶

AIOLI

Makes about 375 ml/13 fl oz

Aioli is a type of mayonnaise which has puréed garlic cloves as a base. It comes from Provence, where it is also sometimes known as '*beurre de Provence*'. An imitation Aioli can be made using bottled or homemade mayonnaise by crushing the garlic and salt, then gradually stirring in the prepared mayonnaise.

INGREDIENTS

6–12 garlic cloves

salt and freshly ground black pepper

2 egg yolks (see page 18)

½–1 tsp Dijon mustard (optional)

about 300 ml/½ pint olive oil

22.5 ml/1½ tbsp lemon juice or white wine vinegar, or a combination of the two

PUT THE GARLIC and a pinch of salt into a mortar or bowl and crush them together until reduced to a paste. Work in the egg yolks, and mustard if using.

Add the oil, a few drops at a time, while stirring slowly, evenly and constantly. After half of the oil has been incorporated, add half of the lemon juice or vinegar. The rest of the oil can now be added a little more quickly but the sauce must be stirred in the same way.

Add the remaining lemon juice or vinegar and season.

DREAMY CALIFORNIA VINAIGRETTE

Makes about 175 ml/6 fl oz

This light dressing partners well with beefsteak tomatoes and most types of salad greens and mushrooms – the fancier the better. Top your salads with this vinaigrette and lots of goat's cheese for a California touch.

INGREDIENTS

2 tbsp chopped fresh coriander

1 tbsp crushed garlic

50 ml/2 fl oz balsamic vinegar

2 tbsp sugar

100 ml/4 fl oz olive oil or light olive oil

salt and freshly ground black pepper

IN A NONREACTIVE BOWL, whisk together the coriander, garlic, vinegar, sugar and oil. Season with salt and pepper to taste. The dressing will keep for about 3 days in the refrigerator.

◀ *Aioli served with fresh bread*

MINT AND TOMATO VINAIGRETTE

Makes about 225 ml/8 fl oz

Quickly make a warm pasta salad with this chunky dressing, or use it to make an interesting
salad out of cooked chicken or turkey. It is also good over salad leaves, with avocado or courgette salads, or served with
warm fish such as tuna, salmon, red mullet or fresh mackerel.

INGREDIENTS

100 ml/3½ fl oz olive oil

5 ml/1 tsp white wine vinegar

7.5 ml/1½ tsp lime juice

1 garlic clove, finely chopped

1 shallot, finely chopped

3 well-flavoured tomatoes

1 tbsp chopped fresh mint

salt and freshly ground black pepper

PUT ALL THE ingredients, except the tomatoes and mint, into a bowl, and whisk together until well emulsified.

Peel, seed and chop the tomatoes. Stir the tomatoes and mint into the dressing and season to taste.

PESTO VINAIGRETTE

Makes about 250 ml/9 fl oz

The addition of pesto sauce quickly makes an interestingly-flavoured dressing that is also versatile; it goes with green, pasta
and nearly all vegetable salads (beetroot is one exception I've found), and with egg, shellfish, chicken, turkey and beef salads.

INGREDIENTS

75–90 ml/5–6 tbsp white wine vinegar

20 ml/4 tsp pesto sauce

150 ml/¼ pint olive oil

salt and freshly ground black pepper

PUT 5 TABLESPOONS of the vinegar and the pesto sauce into a bowl. Slowly pour in the oil, whisking until emulsified.

Season to taste and add more vinegar if liked.

SPECIAL PARSLEY AND LEMON DRESSING

Makes about 175 ml/6 fl oz

If possible, make the dressing a few hours or even a day ahead and leave it in a cool place, preferably not the refrigerator.
Mix again before using in salads with crisp lettuce leaves, such as Cos, and croutons.

INGREDIENTS

150 ml/¼ pint virgin olive oil

30 ml/2 tbsp lemon juice

1 tsp grated lemon zest

2 garlic cloves, finely chopped

2 tsp chopped parsley

5 ml/1 tsp sherry vinegar

1½ tbsp freshly grated Parmesan cheese

salt and freshly ground black pepper

PREPARE THE INGREDIENTS and put them into a bowl. Mix all the ingredients together until well emulsified.

HERB, GARLIC AND MUSTARD DRESSING

Makes about 250 ml/9 fl oz

This is a quite strongly flavoured dressing so is best used for more robust salads such as *salade Niçoise*.

INGREDIENTS

1–2 garlic cloves

salt and freshly ground black pepper

leaves from 4–5 sprigs of thyme

leaves and fine stems from a small bunch of chervil

1 tsp Dijon mustard

50 ml/2 fl oz red wine vinegar

175 ml/6 fl oz olive oil

PUT THE GARLIC, a pinch of salt and herbs into a bowl. Crush together, then stir in the mustard and the vinegar until smooth.

Slowly pour in the oil, whisking constantly, until well emulsified. Season with black pepper.

BASIL DRESSING

Makes about 175 ml/6 fl oz

I love basil but, as it is always at its best when it has basked in glorious
sunshine, I reserve making this dressing until the summer. Then I use it for many salads, such as
warm pasta, shellfish, green, potato, courgette, egg, cheese and grilled vegetables.

INGREDIENTS

2 garlic cloves

leaves from 1 large bunch of basil

salt and freshly ground black pepper

15 ml/1 tbsp white wine

90 ml/6 tbsp virgin olive oil

2 tbsp freshly grated Parmesan cheese

PUT THE GARLIC, basil leaves, pinch of salt and vinegar into a small blender. Mix briefly then, with the motor running, slowly pour in the oil until well emulsified.

Transfer to a bowl. Stir in the cheese and season with black pepper.

CORIANDER, CAPER AND LIME DRESSING

Makes about 225 ml/8 fl oz

Try tossing this piquant dressing with warm potatoes or celeriac then leaving to cool,
or use for seafood salads, or spoon over fried foods such as fish or sliced cheeses such as haloumi or feta.

INGREDIENTS

1 garlic clove, finely chopped

1½ tsp wholegrain mustard

finely grated rind and juice of 2 limes

15 ml/1 tbsp white wine vinegar

60 ml/4 tbsp virgin olive oil

3–4 tbsp capers

3 tbsp chopped fresh coriander

freshly ground black pepper

PUT THE GARLIC, mustard, lime rind and juice and vinegar into a bowl and mix together. Slowly pour in the oil, whisking constantly, until well emulsified. Stir in the capers and coriander. Season with black pepper.

MAYONNAISE-BASED DRESSINGS

HOMEMADE MAYONNAISE

Makes about 175 ml/6 fl oz

Emulsifying this versatile dressing by hand can take patience and a strong wrist, but a tasty version can be made quickly in a food processor or blender. If you substitute pasteurized egg product for the whole egg and use light olive or vegetable oil, you can reduce cholesterol, fat and calories, in addition to eliminating any concerns about the safety of using raw eggs.

INGREDIENTS

1 egg (see page 18), or equivalent egg product

1 tsp dry mustard

pinch of cayenne pepper

1 tsp sugar

100 ml/4 fl oz olive or vegetable oil

45 ml/3 tbsp lemon juice

salt

IN A FOOD processor or blender, combine the egg or egg product, dry mustard, cayenne pepper, sugar and 50 ml/2 fl oz of the oil. Process on a high speed for 1 minute. Add the lemon juice and blend on high again for 10 seconds. Turn the food processor or blender to low, and add the remaining oil, a little at a time, until thick. Add salt to taste, and serve or store in the refrigerator.

GREEN GODDESS DRESSING

Makes about 450 ml/¾ pint

Created in San Francisco, this dressing is named for a popular 1930 movie. Anchovy gives the dressing its kick, while the chives or spring onions and parsley impart the lovely green colour. Serve on any combination of salad greens, or tossed with pasta or potatoes. You may like to use low-fat or non-fat mayonnaise and soured cream to reduce fat and calories.

INGREDIENTS

225 ml/8 fl oz homemade mayonnaise or a commercial variety

1 garlic clove, finely chopped

3 anchovy fillets, drained on kitchen paper towel and finely chopped

25 g/1 oz snipped chives or finely chopped spring onion

15 g/½ oz finely chopped fresh parsley

15 ml/1 tbsp lemon juice

15 ml/1 tbsp tarragon vinegar

100 ml/4 fl oz soured cream

WHISK TOGETHER THE mayonnaise, garlic, anchovy, chives or spring onions, parsley, lemon juice, vinegar and soured cream in a medium bowl to combine well. The dressing will keep for about 3 days in the refrigerator.

ROAST CHILLI AND SZECHUAN PEPPERCORN MAYONNAISE

Makes 325 ml/11 fl oz

This dressing is not as thick as ordinary mayonnaise. It can be used to lend an oriental flavour to all manner of salads.

INGREDIENTS

115 g/4 oz fresh red chillies

2 egg yolks (see page 18)

1 plump garlic clove

salt

30 ml/2 tbsp orange juice

225 ml/8 fl oz mild olive oil (or 115 ml/4 fl oz olive oil and 115 ml/4 fl oz groundnut oil)

pinch of roasted Szechuan peppercorns

PREHEAT THE GRILL. Grill the chillies until the skins are charred and blistered. Leave to cool, then peel off the skins, slice in half, and discard the seeds.

Put the chillies, egg yolks, garlic, salt and orange juice into a blender. Mix together briefly. With the motor running, slowly trickle in the oil. Add Szechuan pepper to taste.

SIMPLE FLAVOURED MAYONNAISES

EXTRA LIGHT MAYONNAISE
Whisk 1–2 egg whites until they form stiff peaks then fold into 350 ml/12 fl oz homemade or bottled mayonnaise.

LIGHT MAYONNAISE
Stir together yogurt and homemade or bottled mayonnaise in the proportions you want. I particularly like to use Greek yogurt for this.

LEMON MAYONNAISE
If making homemade mayonnaise use lemon juice rather than vinegar, and add 2 tablespoons finely grated lemon rind to the egg yolks. If using bottled mayonnaise, add the grated lemon rind to the mayonnaise.

WATERCRESS MAYONNAISE
Remove the tough stalks from a bunch of watercress. Chop the leaves and fine stems and add to 350 ml/ 12 fl oz homemade or bottled mayonnaise.

CHANTILLY MAYONNAISE
Whip 75 ml/3 fl oz whipping or double cream until it stands in soft peaks then gently fold into 350 ml/12 fl oz homemade or bottled mayonnaise.

HORSERADISH MAYONNAISE
Add 15–30 ml/1–2 tablespoons lemon juice and 2 tablespoons freshly grated horseradish to 350 ml/ 12 fl oz homemade or bottled mayonnaise.

HERB MAYONNAISE
Add about 6 tablespoons chopped fresh herbs to 350 ml/12 fl oz homemade or bottled mayonnaise.

CAPER MAYONNAISE
Add 4 teaspoons chopped capers and 1 teaspoon tarragon vinegar to 350 ml/12 fl oz homemade or bottled mayonnaise.

SAUCE VERTE

Makes about 350 ml/12 fl oz

A favourite dressing for cold summer platters of fish, especially salmon, or poultry. The dressing also complements hard-boiled eggs and many cold, boiled vegetables. I use it in egg and chicken sandwiches.

INGREDIENTS

115 g/4 oz mixed herbs and leaves, such as sorrel, watercress and spinach

350 ml/12 fl oz bottled or homemade mayonnaise

◀ *Watercress Mayonnaise*

ADD THE HERBS and leaves to a saucepan of boiling water and boil for 30 seconds. Drain and rinse under cold running water. Drain well and squeeze dry.

Chop finely or purée in a blender. Add the herbs and leaves to the mayonnaise. Cover and chill.

ROAST GARLIC MAYONNAISE

Makes about 350 ml/12 fl oz

Roasting garlic softens its flavour and gives it a delicious smoky taste, which, in turn, adds an enticing flavour to the mayonnaise. If liked, two mashed anchovy fillets can be added with the egg yolks.

INGREDIENTS

2 garlic bulbs, unpeeled

2 sprigs of thyme or rosemary

30 ml/2 tbsp olive oil

2 egg yolks (see page 18)

10–15 ml/2–3 tsp lemon juice

300 ml/½ pint virgin olive oil

salt and freshly ground black pepper

PREHEAT THE OVEN to 180°C/350°F/ Gas Mark 4. Put each garlic bulb on a piece of greaseproof paper. Add a thyme or rosemary sprig and trickle over 1 tablespoon of olive oil. Fold up the greaseproof paper to enclose the garlic and seal the edges together firmly to seal well. Put on a baking sheet and bake for 35–40 minutes until the garlic is soft. Allow the garlic to cool slightly.

Squeeze the garlic cloves from their skins, into a bowl. Add the egg yolks and 1 teaspoon of the lemon juice. Beat hard.

Beat in a drop of virgin olive oil at a time until half of the oil has been added. Add another teaspoon of lemon juice then slowly trickle in the remaining oil, beating hard, constantly.

Season and add more lemon juice, if necessary.

SAFFRON MAYONNAISE

Makes about 350 ml/12 fl oz

Saffron is expensive but only a few strands are needed to make this luxurious-tasting mayonnaise. It adds a real sense of occasion whenever it is used with shellfish salads, for example. To make saffron mayonnaise from bottled mayonnaise, use 1 tablespoon lemon juice and prepare the saffron in the same way. Add to bottled garlic mayonnaise.

INGREDIENTS

30 ml/2 tbsp white wine vinegar

pinch of saffron strands

2 egg yolks (see page 18)

1 garlic clove

salt and freshly ground black pepper

300 ml/½ pint olive oil

POUR THE VINEGAR into a small saucepan. Boil for 2 minutes. Add the saffron, remove from the heat and leave to infuse for 5 minutes.

Put the egg yolks, saffron liquid, garlic and a pinch of salt into a blender. Mix together. With the motor running, slowly trickle in the oil until well emulsified. Season with black pepper.

Ingredients for Roast Garlic Mayonnaise ▶

GINGER AND SPRING ONION MAYONNAISE

Makes about 300 ml/½ pint

To make the ginger juice needed for this recipe, crush a piece of peeled ginger in a garlic press.
Use to dress chicken, pork, fish or shellfish, and vegetable salads.

INGREDIENTS

2 egg yolks (see page 18)

salt

2.5–5 ml/½–1 tsp ginger juice

115 ml/4 fl oz olive oil

115 ml/4 fl oz peanut oil

2 tbsp chopped spring onions

freshly ground black pepper

PUT THE EGG yolks, salt and ½ teaspoon of ginger juice into a blender. Mix briefly. With the motor running, slowly trickle in the oils; add the spring onions almost at the end so they become finely chopped but are not reduced to a pulp.

Season with black pepper. Add more ginger juice if necessary.

PIQUANT CORIANDER MAYONNAISE

Makes about 300 ml/½ pint

I like to serve this delightful dressing with jumbo prawns, crab, lobster, chicken, potato, egg or avocado salads
or with grilled or fried lamb or fish and fish cakes.

INGREDIENTS

1 egg (see page 18)

1 small garlic clove

½ tsp English mustard powder

salt and freshly ground black pepper

175 ml/6 fl oz mild olive oil

4 small cornichons (continental gherkins), finely chopped

1½ tbsp small capers

1 tbsp chopped fresh coriander

10 ml/2 tsp lime juice

PUT THE EGG, garlic, mustard powder and seasoning into a blender. Mix briefly, then with the motor still running, very slowly trickle in the oil. Transfer the sauce to a bowl and stir in the remaining ingredients.

◀ *Ginger and Spring Onion Mayonnaise*

SESAME SEED AND GARLIC MAYONNAISE

Makes about 325 ml/11 fl oz

Rice vinegar is used for this recipe so the dressing is mild, getting its character from the spring onions,
roasted sesame seeds and a little garlic (you can increase the garlic if liked). To roast sesame seeds, put them into a dry,
heavy, small frying pan and heat gently until they are light brown in colour and smell toasted.

INGREDIENTS

2 egg yolks (see page 18)
2 garlic cloves
salt
10 ml/2 tsp white rice vinegar

225 ml/8 fl oz mild olive oil (or 115 ml/4 fl oz olive oil and 115 ml/4 fl oz peanut oil)
4 tbsp chopped spring onions
1 tbsp sesame seeds, roasted
freshly ground black pepper

PUT THE EGG yolks, garlic, salt and white rice vinegar into a blender. Mix together briefly. With the motor running, slowly trickle in the olive oil; spring onions almost at the end.

Transfer to a bowl. Fold in the sesame seeds and season with black pepper.

CURRY MAYONNAISE

Makes about 225 ml/8 fl oz

Use for chicken, ham, egg or potato salads, to liven up left over roast turkey, or in chicken, ham or egg sandwiches.

INGREDIENTS

90 ml/6 tbsp bottled or homemade mayonnaise
90 ml/6 tbsp double cream
15 ml/1 tbsp curry paste
1 tbsp finely chopped shallot or red onion
juice of ½ lemon
1 tbsp mango chutney
salt and freshly ground black pepper

PUT ALL THE ingredients into a bowl and stir together until well mixed. Cover and leave to stand for at least 30 minutes before serving.

Sesame Seed and Garlic Mayonnaise ▶

COLESLAW DRESSING

Makes about 325 ml/11 fl oz

Caraway seeds, a classic complement to cabbage, give this creamy dressing an extra touch of distinction.

INGREDIENTS

115 ml/4 fl oz soured cream

115 ml/4 fl oz mayonnaise, bottled or homemade

75 ml/5 tbsp cider vinegar

1 tsp mustard powder

2 tsp caraway seeds

pinch of caster sugar

salt and freshly ground black pepper

PUT THE SOURED cream, mayonnaise, vinegar, mustard powder and caraway seeds in a bowl. Whisk together until evenly combined. Add sugar and seasoning to taste.

REMOULADE SAUCE

Makes about 450 ml/15 fl oz

This robustly-flavoured recipe is for the classic remoulade sauce, which really adds life to cold meats, eggs, fish and boiled vegetables, turning them into appetizing salads. As an alternative you could mix in celeriac, mustard and lemon juice to make celeriac remoulade.

INGREDIENTS

350 ml/12 fl oz mayonnaise, bottled or homemade

2 tsp Dijon mustard

3 tbsp pickled gherkins, chopped

3 tbsp capers, chopped

3 tbsp chopped fresh parsley

1 tbsp chopped fresh tarragon

4 anchovy fillets, chopped

PUT THE MAYONNAISE into a bowl. Prepare the remaining ingredients and add to the mayonnaise. Stir well until thoroughly mixed.

◀ *Coleslaw Dressing*

DRESSINGS WITH YOGURT, CHEESE & CREAM

WARM MINTED LEMON CREAM DRESSING

Makes about 175 ml/6 fl oz

To make a cold dressing, simply stir all the ingredients together. This is an ideal dressing for young, sweet peas, sugar snap peas, baby carrots and baby sweetcorn.

INGREDIENTS

60 ml/4 tbsp crème fraîche

finely grated rind and juice of ½ lemon

1 tbsp finely chopped or shredded fresh mint

75 ml/5 tbsp plain yogurt

salt and freshly ground black pepper

PUT THE CRÈME fraîche into a small saucepan and heat gently. Stir in the lemon rind and juice, and the mint. When warmed through, stir in the yogurt, taking care not to let the dressing overheat. Season to taste.

YOGURT VINAIGRETTE

Makes about 350 ml/12 fl oz

This is a lighter tasting, fresher alternative to ordinary vinaigrette, and can be used in the same way. Walnut or hazelnut oil can be substituted for half of the olive oil, depending on the salad.

INGREDIENTS

90 ml/6 tbsp plain yogurt

30 ml/2 tbsp sherry vinegar

60 ml/4 tbsp olive oil

2 tsp Dijon mustard

about 30 ml/2 tbsp water (optional)

pinch of caster sugar

salt and freshly ground white or black pepper

PUT THE YOGURT, vinegar, oil and mustard into a bowl and mix together. If the vinaigrette is too thick (thicknesses of yogurts vary), add a little water. Add sugar and seasoning to taste.

YOGURT SALAD DRESSING

Makes about 325 ml/11 fl oz

An easy to make, light, fresh tasting dressing that will liven up green salads. The dressing will not keep very long as the yogurt acts on the cream and turns it into rich yogurt.

INGREDIENTS

150 ml/¼ pint plain yogurt

150 ml/¼ pint double cream

juice of 1 lemon

pinch of caster sugar

salt and freshly ground white or black pepper

Put the yogurt, cream and lemon juice into a bowl and stir together. Add sugar and seasoning to taste.

MUSTARD YOGURT DRESSING

Makes about 300 ml/½ pint

A light but well-flavoured dressing for spinach, potato or other vegetable salads.

INGREDIENTS

225 ml/8 fl oz plain yogurt

1 tbsp finely chopped spring onion

1 tbsp Dijon mustard

1 tbsp chopped fresh parsley or chives

salt and pepper

PUT ALL THE ingredients into a bowl and stir together until evenly mixed. Cover and chill before using.

LIGHT HERB SAUCE

Makes about 175 ml/6 fl oz

A simple, quick sauce that can be flavoured with any herb. If you prefer a milder dressing, leave out the shallot. Serve the dressing over green salads, warm new potato salads, vegetable salads, or warm white beans such as haricot or cannellini.

INGREDIENTS

150 ml/¼ pint soured cream, Greek yogurt or plain yogurt

2 tbsp chopped fresh herbs

1 tsp finely chopped shallot

salt and freshly ground white or black pepper

PUT THE SOURED cream or yogurt, herbs and shallot into a bowl. Stir together and season to taste.

HERBY CREAM CHEESE DRESSING

Makes scant 300 ml/½ pint

Mixing buttermilk with soft cheese makes a dressing that is creamy but not too rich. The fresh flavours of the herbs also make it taste light. Use it for cooked vegetable salads or salads containing chicken.

INGREDIENTS

115 g/4 oz full fat soft cheese

150 ml/¼ pint buttermilk

5–10 ml/1–2 tsp lemon juice

4 tbsp chopped fresh mixed herbs or 2 tbsp chopped fresh tarragon or basil

salt and freshly ground black pepper

PUT THE SOFT cheese into a bowl. Slowly pour in the buttermilk, stirring, until evenly blended. Add the lemon juice. Mix in the herbs. Season to taste. Serve chilled.

◄ *Mustard Yogurt Dressing*

CREAMY MUSTARD VINAIGRETTE

Makes about 125 ml/4½ fl oz

Tarragon and fennel seeds give complexity to the flavour of this powerful dressing, while
crème fraîche smooths the flavour with piquant creaminess. The vinaigrette is great over white bean and robust
lettuce leaf salads, potato salads, cheese salads, eggs or with beef.

INGREDIENTS

¼ tsp fennel seeds

1 tsp tarragon leaves

½ tsp Dijon mustard

22.5 ml/1½ tbsp sherry vinegar

salt

30 ml/2 tbsp crème fraîche or
soured cream

90 ml/6 tbsp olive oil

PUT THE FENNEL seeds into a bowl and crush with the end of a rolling-pin. Add the tarragon and crush lightly.

Stir the Dijon mustard, sherry vinegar, salt and crème fraîche into the bowl. Slowly pour in the oil, whisking until well emulsified.

CREAMY WATERCRESS DRESSING

Makes about 175 ml/6 fl oz

You can use all double cream or crème fraîche, or dilute either with some yogurt in whatever
proportions you like, but keep at least 2 tablespoons of cream or crème fraîche for some creaminess and body.
Alternatively, use Greek yogurt for a creamy taste but not too many calories. Soured cream could also be used. Serve
over pulse, rice or potato salads, with cold salmon, trout, chicken or eggs, or in egg sandwiches.

INGREDIENTS

large handful of watercress leaves

150 ml/¼ pint double cream or crème
fraîche, or a mixture of either plain
yogurt, Greek yogurt or soured cream

squeeze of lemon juice (optional)

salt and freshly ground white
or black pepper

ADD THE WATERCRESS leaves to a saucepan of boiling water and boil for 1 minute. Drain and rinse under running cold water. Drain well and dry thoroughly.

Put the watercress into a blender and add the cream, crème fraîche and/or yogurt or soured cream. Mix to a green purée. Season to taste.

YOGURT AND CURD CHEESE "MAYONNAISE"

Makes about 150 ml/¼ pint

The taste of this low-fat version of mayonnaise is not too far removed from the real thing.
It can be flavoured in the same way as mayonnaise with garlic, mustard, herbs etc, and served in place of mayonnaise.
A little milk can be added to thin the mayonnaise if liked.

INGREDIENTS

115 g/4 oz medium fat curd cheese or medium fat soft cheese

30 ml/2 tbsp plain yogurt

10 ml/2 tsp olive oil

2.5 ml/½ tsp white wine vinegar

salt and freshly ground black pepper

PUT THE CHEESE into a bowl. Stir in the yogurt, oil and vinegar until smooth. Season to taste. Chill before serving.

HORSERADISH AND SOURED CREAM DRESSING

Makes about 200 ml/7 fl oz

Spoon this dressing over sliced tomatoes, toss with boiled cauliflower for an inspired salad, or serve with sliced cold beef.

INGREDIENTS

175 ml/6 fl oz soured cream

4 tbsp grated fresh or bottled horseradish

10 ml/2 tsp lemon juice or white wine vinegar

salt and freshly ground black pepper

POUR THE SOURED cream into a bowl. Stir in the horseradish and lemon juice or white wine vinegar. Season to taste. Cover and chill.

RICOTTA AND BLUE CHEESE DRESSING

Makes about 425 ml/15 fl oz

A cheese with some piquancy is best for this dressing to contrast with the creaminess of the ricotta cheese.
The dressing can be flavoured with garlic, spring onions, or herbs such as parsley, rosemary or sage. Use for warm pasta,
potato, rice, butter or cannellini beans, or green lentil salads, or over crisp lettuce leaves.

INGREDIENTS

150 g/5 oz ricotta cheese

150 g/5 oz Stilton or other blue cheese
such as Gorgonzola or Roquefort

150 g/5 oz crème fraîche

salt and fresh ground black pepper

CRUMBLE THE RICOTTA and blue cheese into a bowl and mash lightly together with a fork. Slowly pour in the crème fraîche, mixing well with a fork until the dressing is smooth. Season with a little salt and plenty of black pepper.

TOFU MAYONNAISE

Makes about 175 ml/6 fl oz

This delicious, creamy mayonnaise-style dressing is useful for vegans.
It can be flavoured with a little crushed garlic, some chopped herbs or a few drops of chilli sauce.
This mayonnaise can be kept in a covered container in the refrigerator for a few days.

INGREDIENTS

115 g/4 oz silken tofu

10 ml/2 tsp lemon juice

1 tsp Dijon mustard

30 ml/2 tbsp sunflower oil

salt and freshly ground black pepper

PUT ALL THE ingredients into a blender and mix until smooth. Prepare ingredients for flavouring and add to mayonnaise, stirring until mixed (optional).

Ricotta and Blue Cheese Dressing ▶

OIL-FREE CREAM VINAIGRETTE

Makes about 300 ml/½ pint

Chill the dressing well and pour it over crisp lettuce leaves, or mix with cold cooked vegetables. Do not make the dressing too far in advance otherwise the vinegar will act upon the cream and thicken it.

INGREDIENTS

½ garlic clove

salt and freshly ground white or black pepper

1 hard-boiled egg

½ tsp Dijon mustard

10 ml/2 tsp tarragon vinegar

225 ml/8 fl oz single cream

pinch of caster sugar

Put the garlic into a mortar or a bowl, add a pinch of salt, and crush together to a paste.

Separate the egg white from the yolk; reserve the egg white for garnishing the salad. Add the egg yolk, mustard and vinegar to the bowl and mix with the garlic. Stir in the cream and add sugar and pepper to taste. Cover and chill.

YOGURT AND TAHINI DRESSING

Makes about 200 ml/7 fl oz

I have had various versions of this dressing throughout the Middle East.
Sometimes the ground cumin is omitted, sometimes chopped coriander or paprika are added. Serve it with
egg salads, as a dressing for coleslaw salad, with warm new potatoes, or crudités.

INGREDIENTS

15–20 ml/3–4 tsp lemon juice

90 ml/6 tbsp plain yogurt

1–2 garlic cloves, finely crushed

90 ml/6 tbsp olive oil

4 tbsp tahini

pinch of ground cumin

salt and freshly ground black pepper

Whisk the lemon juice into the yogurt. Add the garlic. Slowly stir in the oil until well mixed.

Beat in the tahini then add ground cumin and seasoning to taste. Cover and chill before using.

YOGURT AND ORANGE DRESSING

Makes about 300 ml/½ pint

Use for first course fruit salads, such as melon and orange, and garnish with mint.

INGREDIENTS

45 ml/3 tbsp orange juice

15 ml/1 tbsp clear honey

225 ml/8 fl oz thick plain yogurt

salt and freshly ground white pepper

STIR THE ORANGE juice into the honey. Add the orange juice mixture to the yogurt and stir together. Season to taste. Cover and chill.

CONFETTI RANCH DRESSING

Makes about 300 ml/½ pint

This topping is a cool, refreshing treat when poured over crunchy salad greens or drizzled on melon or a combination of grated raw turnips and red grapes. Use low-fat or non-fat yogurt to cut calories, if desired.

INGREDIENTS

1 large garlic clove, crushed into a paste with a knife, pestle and mortar, or garlic press

30 ml/2 tbsp olive oil

225 ml/8 fl oz yogurt

1 red pepper, finely chopped

1 green pepper, finely chopped

1 yellow pepper, finely chopped

½ tsp cumin

¼ tsp dried cayenne or hot pepper sauce

½ tsp finely chopped fresh coriander (optional)

salt and freshly ground black pepper

PLACE THE GARLIC, olive oil, yogurt, peppers, cumin, cayenne or hot pepper sauce, and coriander in a medium bowl and mix together to combine. Season with salt and pepper to taste. Chill in the refrigerator for 2–24 hours. The dressing will keep in the refrigerator for about 3 days.

MINT-RICOTTA SMOOTHIE DRESSING

Makes about 350 ml/12 fl oz

This creamy blend is wonderful on fresh fruit, particularly melons, berries, peaches, apples or pears. Ricotta is creamy without being high in dairy fat, so enjoy this topping without fretting about pounds.

INGREDIENTS

300 g/11 oz light ricotta cheese

4 tbsp finely chopped fresh mint

60–90 ml/4–6 tbsp freshly squeezed or bottled lime juice

3 tsp caster sugar

PLACE THE RICOTTA cheese in a food processor or blender and purée for 2 minutes until smooth. Transfer to a bowl. Stir in the mint, lime juice and sugar. The dressing will keep for about 3 days in the refrigerator.

Confetti Ranch Dressing ▶

FISH & SEAFOOD SALADS

LEMON AND LIME SEAFOOD SALAD

Serves 4–6

This is a fresh-tasting fish salad. The choice of fish and herbs can be varied according to taste.

INGREDIENTS

450 g/1 lb fresh haddock

2 fresh scallops

225 g/8 oz monkfish or huss

175 g/6 oz prepared fresh squid

175 g/6 oz fresh peeled prawns

6 tbsp chopped fresh parsley

2 tbsp chopped fresh tarragon

4 tbsp chopped fresh mint

45 ml/3 tbsp olive oil

juice of 1 lemon

juice of 1 lime

bunch of spring onions, trimmed and chopped

salt and freshly ground pepper

CLEAN AND SKIN the haddock and cut into small pieces. Clean the scallops. Bone and cube the monkfish or huss. Wash the squid and cut into rings. Poach all together in lightly salted water for a short time until just cooked. Drain well, cool, and place in a mixing bowl with the peeled prawns.

Place all the herbs in a bowl with the oil, citrus juices, spring onions, salt and freshly ground pepper. Stir round and pour over the fish and lightly toss. Leave for approximately 30 minutes for the flavours to develop.

Serve with a rice salad and sliced tomatoes and, if liked, garlic bread.

CITRUSY FRENCH DRESSING

Makes about 175 ml/6 fl oz

This recipe makes a refreshing dressing for all sorts of seafood salads, such as prawn, lobster, squid and tuna.

INGREDIENTS

45 ml/3 tbsp fresh or bottled lemon or lime juice

½ tsp salt

⅛ tsp black pepper

¼ tsp sugar

¼ tsp dry mustard (optional)

100 ml/4 fl oz olive, sesame or rapeseed oil

PLACE THE LEMON or lime juice, salt, black pepper, sugar and dry mustard in a food processor or blender and blend on high until mixed.

Add the oil 5 ml/1 tsp at a time until well combined.

Alternatively, whisk all the ingredients together, except the oil, in a small bowl, then add the oil a little at a time, whisking continuously until the oil is incorporated.

◀ *Lemon and Lime Seafood Salad*

HUNGARIAN HERRING SALAD

Serves 4–6

Some of the most wonderful herring dishes come from Hungary, where fish has been pickled for centuries.
The apples add a touch of sweetness and a crunchy texture.

INGREDIENTS

2 pickled herrings

3 hard-boiled eggs

2 medium boiled potatoes

2 red apples, cored and seeded

1 tbsp chopped onion

50 ml/2 fl oz vinegar

50 ml/2 fl oz olive oil

½ tsp prepared mustard

salt

mild sweet paprika

SLICE THE PICKLED herrings into small pieces, and place in a large serving dish. Dice the hard-boiled eggs, potatoes and apples, and add to the dish with the chopped onion. In a small bowl, blend the vinegar, olive oil and mustard together, and season to taste with the salt and paprika. Pour over the salad, and toss gently to coat. Leave to stand for 30 minutes before serving, then sprinkle with a little paprika to add a dash of colour.

LUSCIOUS LOBSTER SALAD

Serves 4

Using white pepper in the court bouillon and the vinaigrette maintains the pristine look of the velvety, white lobster meat in this adaptation of a classic French salad.

INGREDIENTS

2 lobsters, about 575 g/1¼ lb each

175–225 g/6–8 oz torn mixed salad greens

COURT BOUILLON

2 carrots, scrubbed and sliced

2 celery stalks, sliced

1 leek, sliced

1 sprig of fresh thyme

1 bay leaf

1 tsp salt

½ tsp white pepper

2 l/3½ pints water

450 ml/¾ pint dry white wine

FRUIT VINAIGRETTE

90 ml/6 tbsp walnut oil

50 ml/2 fl oz balsamic vinegar

½ mango or 4 fresh peaches, diced

2 shallots, diced, or
2 tbsp chopped red onion

25 g/1 oz red pepper, diced

7–15 g/¼–½ oz whole coriander leaves

salt and white pepper

Place all the court bouillon ingredients in a tall saucepan. Bring to the boil over a high heat and continue to boil for 20 minutes. Add the lobsters to the pan and return to the boil for 12 minutes, until the shells have turned bright red. Using tongs, remove the lobsters from the pan. The bouillon can be reserved for use in a seafood stew or another dish. When the lobsters are cool enough to handle, remove the meat from the claws and tail. To do this, twist off the claws and crack them to extract the meat. For each lobster, separate the tail from the head and body. Cut down the centre length of the underside of the tail, bend apart and remove the meat. Discard the head and body. Slice the tail meat crossways, and set aside.

Make the vinaigrette by mixing the walnut oil, balsamic vinegar, mango or peaches, shallots or onion, pepper and coriander leaves in a small bowl. Season with salt and white pepper to taste, and set aside.

Divide the salad greens between four plates and spoon three-quarters of the vinaigrette over them. Arrange the lobster meat on top of the greens, spoon over the remaining vinaigrette, and serve.

SALMON MOUSSE

Serves 4

Some of the best sockeye, or red, salmon comes from British Columbia's Fraser River and Alaska's Copper River.

INGREDIENTS

½ x 225 g/8-oz can sockeye salmon, drained

2.25 ml/1½ tbsp lemon juice

100 ml/4 fl oz soured cream

100 g/4 oz cream cheese, softened

50 ml/2 fl oz mayonnaise

22.5 ml/1½ tbsp chilli sauce

⅛ tsp hot pepper sauce

5 ml/1 tsp Worcestershire sauce

¼ tsp salt

¼ tsp white pepper

1 x 7-g/¼-oz envelope gelatine

22.5 ml/1½ tbsp cold water

50 ml/2 fl oz boiling water

25 g/1 oz green pepper, finely chopped

25 g/1 oz celery, finely chopped

25 g/1 oz spring onions, finely chopped

butter, for greasing

parsley sprigs, to garnish

REMOVE ANY SKIN and bones from the salmon. Sprinkle the salmon with the lemon juice, and set aside.

In a food processor, or with an electric mixer, combine the soured cream, cream cheese and mayonnaise. Add chilli sauce, hot pepper sauce, Worcestershire sauce, salt and white pepper. Mix well and set aside.

Soften the gelatine in the cold water, then add boiling water and stir to dissolve the gelatine. Leave to cool, then add to the cream cheese mixture in food processor and mix well. Add the salmon to the food processor until just combined. Fold in the pepper, celery and spring onions.

Pour into a greased 1.75–3-pint mould. Cover and refrigerate overnight. Turn out of the mould and garnish with parsley sprigs.

JAPANESE PRAWN SALAD

Serves 4

Here is a prawn salad with the tastes and textures of Japanese cuisine.

INGREDIENTS

350 g/12 oz bean sprouts

1 bunch watercress, washed with
tough stalks discarded

8 large cooked and chilled prawns,
shelled and cut into quarters

2 tbsp crushed toasted sesame seeds

30 ml/2 tbsp soy sauce

15 ml/1 tbsp vinegar

15 ml/1 tbsp sesame oil

1 tsp sugar

HALF-FILL A large saucepan with water. Bring to the boil over a high heat. Drop in the bean sprouts and cook for 30 seconds. Drain, rinse with cold water and drain again. Cover and refrigerate until cold.

Tear the watercress into 5-cm/2-in lengths, and place in a serving bowl with the bean sprouts, prawns and sesame seeds. Stir the soy sauce, vinegar, sesame oil and sugar together in a small bowl. Pour over the salad, toss until well coated, and serve.

LUXURIOUS CRAB LOUIS

Serves 4

Food writer, historian and biographer Evan Jones has traced this salad to Solari's, a San Francisco restaurant that served it as early as 1914. This dish is luxurious, combining rich-tasting crabmeat, artichokes and cream.

INGREDIENTS

½ iceberg lettuce, shredded, or shredded mixed lettuces

about 450 g/1 lb flaked fresh crabmeat

225 ml/8 fl oz homemade mayonnaise

75 ml/5 tbsp whipped cream

10 ml/2 tsp Worcestershire sauce

1 tsp chopped fresh dill

30–45 ml/2–3 tbsp chilli sauce

2–3 tbsp grated onion

25 g/1 oz green pepper, chopped

1–3 tbsp chopped fresh parsley

cayenne pepper

3–4 hard-boiled eggs, quartered

3–4 tomatoes, cut into wedges

6–8 small bottled artichoke hearts, or frozen artichoke hearts, thawed

DIVIDE THE LETTUCE among four plates. Place one-quarter of the crabmeat on top of lettuce on each plate. In a small bowl, mix the mayonnaise with the cream, Worcestershire sauce, dill, chilli sauce, onion, green pepper and parsley, and add cayenne pepper to taste. Spread one-quarter liberally over the crabmeat on each plate and top with eggs, tomato wedges and artichokes.

TRES COLORES CEVICHE DE MEXICO

Serves 4

This tri-coloured salad, influenced by Mexican cuisine, is bright with yellow, red and green peppers. The snapper is cured by the acidic lime and lemon juices. If you are worried about uncooked seafood, poach or steam the snapper first, then chill the fish, and proceed with the recipe.

INGREDIENTS

675 g/1½ lb red snapper fillets

¼ tsp pickling salt

½ tsp freshly ground black pepper

1 large red pepper,
cut into very thin rings

1 large green pepper,
cut into very thin rings

1 large yellow pepper,
cut into very thin rings

1 red onion, very thinly sliced

225 ml/8 fl oz fresh lemon juice

100 ml/4 fl oz fresh lime juice

45 ml/3 tbsp tequila

unsalted butter

kosher salt

2 tbsp chopped fresh coriander,
to garnish

REMOVE THE SKIN from the snapper fillets and arrange a single layer of the snapper fillets in a large glass dish. Season with the pickling salt and freshly ground black pepper. Cover with the thinly sliced pepper rings and onion slices. Pour the lemon juice, lime juice and tequila over it, and cover with plastic wrap. Marinate in the refrigerator, turning occasionally, for about 36 hours, until the fish is almost opaque.

Rub a small amount of butter around the rims of four glass serving plates. Roll the rims in kosher salt, as you would a margarita glass. Place the plates in the refrigerator for about 5 minutes, until the salted rims harden.

Drain the snapper and cut it into 2.5-cm/1-in cubes. Arrange one-quarter of the pepper and onion rings on each plate, then mound one-quarter of the fish in the centre of each plate. Garnish with coriander and serve.

SOUTH AMERICAN MUSSEL SALAD

Serves 4

Buy mussels with tightly closed shells or shells that close tightly when tapped. Gaping shells indicate that the shellfish are dead and definitely not edible. Keep the mussels cold until you are ready to prepare them. The mussels can be served in their shells if preferred.

INGREDIENTS

2.5 kg/5½ lb mussels

salt

bicarbonate of soda or flour

50 ml/2 fl oz olive oil

75 ml/5 tbsp sherry vinegar

2.5 ml/½ tsp lemon juice

½ garlic clove, peeled and finely chopped

½ serrano or jalapeño chilli, seeded and finely chopped

¼ tsp ground fennel

½ tsp coarse salt

½ medium red onion, peeled and thinly sliced

1 medium fennel bulb, thinly sliced

15 g/½ oz finely chopped flat-leaf parsley

½ tsp finely chopped fresh dill

SCRUB THE MUSSELS with a brush under cold running water to remove all the sand and mud from the shells. Rinse and place in a solution of 5 tablespoons salt per 4 litres/7 pints water with 1 tablespoon bicarbonate of soda or a sprinkling of flour. Leave to soak for about 2 hours. Discard any mussels that float, or are broken or damaged. Rinse again. Pull out and cut off the string beards from each mussel. Drain and set aside.

Place the mussels in a frying pan or sauté pan with a tight-fitting lid, and add 225 ml/8 fl oz water. Cover the saucepan and steam the mussels over high heat for about 5 minutes. Discard any mussels that have not opened. Transfer the mussels to a bowl using a slotted spoon. Discard the liquid. When the mussels are cool enough to handle, gently pull off any remaining beards and remove the mussels, intact, from their shells; discard the shells.

Mix together the olive oil, vinegar, lemon juice, garlic, chilli, ground fennel, salt, onion, fennel and parsley. Toss well and adjust the seasoning by adding salt, if necessary. Add the mussels, toss again and transfer to a serving dish. Sprinkle with the dill and serve.

ANTIPASTO ITALIANO

Serves 4–6

You can embellish this salad by adding other titbits, such as artichoke hearts, tiny onions, green beans or slices of Italian salami and mortadella. You can also use stuffed olives, anchovies, radish roses or pickled onions for garnishing.

INGREDIENTS

50 ml/2 fl oz ketchup

50 ml/2 fl oz chilli sauce

50 ml/2 fl oz water

50 ml/2 fl oz olive oil

50 ml/2 fl oz tarragon wine vinegar

50 ml/2 fl oz fresh lemon juice

¼ garlic clove, finely chopped

½ tbsp brown sugar

7.5 ml/½ tbsp Worcestershire sauce

½ tbsp prepared horseradish

pinch of cayenne pepper

salt

½ small cauliflower, broken into florets

2 carrots, peeled, sliced into 5 mm/¼-in rounds

1 celery stalk, cut into 4-cm/1½-in lengths

100 g/4 oz small whole mushrooms

1 × 100 g/4-oz jar pepperoncini, drained and seeded

1 × 200 g/7-oz can water-packed tuna, drained

25 g/1oz anchovies, drained

12 green olives, sliced

IN A LARGE nonreactive saucepan, combine the ketchup, chilli sauce, water, oil, vinegar, lemon juice, garlic, brown sugar, Worcestershire sauce, horseradish, cayenne pepper and salt to taste. Bring to the boil, then reduce heat and simmer, uncovered, for 2–3 minutes. Add cauliflower florets, carrots, celery, mushrooms and pepperoncini to the pan. Cover, reduce heat, and simmer slowly for about 20 minutes, until the vegetables are tender-crisp when pierced with a fork. Gently add the tuna in large flakes. Simmer, uncovered, until the tuna is just heated. Spoon on to a divided serving dish, keeping each type of vegetable and the tuna separated. Leave to cool, and then refrigerate for 2 hours. Garnish with anchovies and olives, and serve.

MEDITERRANEAN TUNA AND WHITE BEAN SALAD

Serves 4

This wonderful concoction combines the delicate flavour of cannellini beans with tuna. The Italian white kidney beans are available in dry and canned forms. Use the best quality of extra virgin olive oil you can find to ensure successful results.

INGREDIENTS

2 × 190-g/6½-oz cans water-packed tuna, drained and flaked

40 g/1½ oz red onion or spring onions, chopped

4 medium tomatoes, chopped

20 g/¾ oz chopped fresh basil

2 tbsp finely chopped fresh parsley

2 × 425-g/15-oz cans cannellini beans, rinsed and well drained

about 175 g/6 oz cooked pasta shapes or elbow macaroni

Cos lettuce or fresh spinach leaves

DRESSING

4 tbsp capers

75 ml/5 tbsp red wine vinegar

15 ml/1 tbsp balsamic vinegar

2 garlic cloves, crushed

¼ tsp salt

¼ tsp freshly ground black pepper

45–60 ml/3–4 tbsp extra virgin olive oil

IN A JAR with a tight-fitting lid, combine capers, red wine vinegar, balsamic vinegar, garlic, salt, pepper and olive oil. Cover, shake well and set aside for 1–2 hours to let the flavours blend.

In a large serving bowl, combine the tuna, onion, tomatoes, basil, parsley, beans and pasta. Just before serving, pour the dressing over the salad, toss gently to coat, and serve on a bed of lettuce or spinach leaves.

OREGANO AND ANCHOVY DRESSING

Makes about 200 ml/7 fl oz

I suggest using this dressing for grilled aubergines, peppers, courgettes and onions, with tomato or green salads, or with grilled fish. A small blender can also be used to make the dressing: put the soaked anchovy fillets, garlic, herbs and half the lemon juice into the blender or food processor and mix briefly. With the motor running, very slowly trickle in the oil until the dressing is well emulsified. Switch off the machine and add the sun-dried tomatoes and black pepper.

INGREDIENTS

75-g/3-oz can anchovy fillets

a little milk

1 small garlic clove, minced

1½ tbsp finely chopped fresh oregano

juice of 1 lemon

75 ml/5 tbsp virgin olive oil

1 tsp finely chopped sun-dried tomatoes in oil

freshly ground black pepper

SOAK THE ANCHOVY fillets in milk for 5 minutes, then drain. Put the anchovy fillets into a mortar with the garlic and herbs and crush together with a pestle to make a smooth paste, slowly working in half of the lemon juice.

Beat in the oil a drop at a time until half has been added. Stir in the remaining lemon juice then slowly trickle in the remaining oil, beating constantly. Lightly stir in the chopped sun-dried tomatoes and season with black pepper.

NIÇOISE SALAD

Serves 4–6

This famous salad from France makes a wonderful, refreshing lunch or dinner on a warm day.

INGREDIENTS

1 round lettuce

75 ml/6 fl oz French vinaigrette

225 g/8 oz green beans, cooked

225 g/8 oz cooked potatoes, diced

225-g/8-oz can tuna, drained and flaked

2–3 tomatoes, peeled and quartered

2 hard-boiled eggs, quartered

6 anchovies, cut in half

1 tbsp chopped fresh tarragon, chervil, or parsley

WASH AND DRY the lettuce, tear into small pieces, and put in a salad bowl. Sprinkle a few tablespoons of the French dressing over the top. Arrange the beans, potatoes and tuna on top of the salad greens, and place the tomatoes around the edge of the bowl. Top with the eggs and anchovies. Pour over the remaining dressing, sprinkle with fresh tarragon, chervil or parsley, and serve.

◄ *Oregano and Anchovy Dressing*

WARM PRAWN AND SESAME SALAD

Serves 4

This salad combines several textures, colours and flavours. It is served warm to bring out the full toasty, nutty crunchiness of the sesame seeds.

INGREDIENTS

2 heads chicory, cored and leaves separated

1 small radicchio, leaves separated

2 small round lettuce, leaves separated

450 g/1 lb prawns, shelled and deveined with tails left on

15 ml/1 tbsp olive oil

2 tbsp finely chopped spring onions

2 tsp finely chopped garlic

2 tsp grated fresh pared ginger root

spinach leaves

225 g/8 oz cherry tomatoes, halved

4 tbsp toasted sesame seeds

DRESSING

100 ml/4 fl oz dry sherry

45 ml/3 tbsp lemon juice

30 ml/2 tbsp olive oil

1 tbsp sugar

2 garlic cloves, crushed

½ tsp finely chopped fresh rosemary

salt and freshly ground black pepper

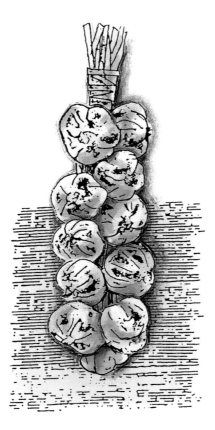

PLACE CHICORY, RADICCHIO, and lettuce in a large salad bowl. Cover and refrigerate until serving time. Make the dressing by combining the sherry, lemon juice, olive oil, sugar, garlic, rosemary and salt and pepper to taste in a jar with a tight-fitting lid and shaking well. Refrigerate until ready to assemble the salad.

Pat the prawns dry with kitchen paper towel. Heat the olive oil in large frying pan over a high heat. Add the prawns and cook, stirring, until just pink and lightly browned. Remove the frying pan from heat and quickly add the spring onions, garlic and ginger. Toss constantly until the spring onions are wilted and the mixture is fragrant. Leave to cool to room temperature.

To serve, line four plates with the spinach leaves. Gently toss the chilled salad greens with the dressing, and divide between the plates. Top each plate with one-quarter of the prawn mixture. Arrange the tomatoes between the plates, and sprinkle the salads with toasted sesame seeds.

SALMON AND POTATO SALAD WITH HORSERADISH DRESSING

Serves 4

Ask your fishmonger to slice the salmon for you, if you feel uneasy about slicing it yourself.

INGREDIENTS

675 g/1½ lb small waxy potatoes

salt

1 large bunch of watercress, cleaned with tough stalks discarded

olive oil cooking spray

350 g/12 oz salmon fillet, cut into thin slices on the diagonal

salt and freshly ground black pepper

HORSERADISH DRESSING

225 g/8 fl oz low-fat buttermilk

2 spring onions, coarsely chopped

25 g/1 oz prepared horseradish, drained

salt and freshly ground black pepper

COVER THE POTATOES with cold water in a medium saucepan and add 1 teaspoon salt. Bring to the boil over a moderately high heat and cook for about 20 minutes, until the potatoes are tender. Drain the potatoes and slice them crossways in 5-mm/¼-in thick slices. When cooled, place the potatoes in a bowl with the watercress leaves.

Make the dressing by stirring the buttermilk, spring onions and horseradish together in a small bowl. Season with salt and pepper to taste. Add half the dressing to the potatoes and watercress, and toss to coat. Arrange the salad on four large plates, and drizzle with the remaining

Lightly coat a grill pan or large nonstick frying pan with cooking spray and heat. Season the salmon with salt and pepper; add to the frying pan, and sear over a high heat, without turning, for about 30 seconds, until browned on the bottom. Remove from the pan or frying pan, and arrange, browned sides up, on the salads. Serve immediately.

HAWAIIAN PRAWN SALAD

Serves 4

This salad draws on Hawaiian cuisine for inspiration. Red pepper juice is a Hawaiian ingredient and can be obtained by extracting the juice from red peppers. If you can find sweet onions, you can garnish the platters with onion rings. The onions have a high sugar content and taste delicious in salads.

INGREDIENTS

100 ml/4 fl oz fresh orange juice

50 ml/2 fl oz fresh lime juice

175 ml/6 fl oz vegetable or almond oil, or red pepper juice with 5 ml/1 tsp almond oil added

salt and freshly ground black pepper

about 175 g/6 oz mixed salad greens, torn into small pieces and chilled

2 christophene, peeled and cut into julienne strips

225 g/8 oz cooked prawns, shelled

2 tbsp capers

sweet onion rings, to garnish (optional)

IN A SMALL saucepan, boil the orange and lime juices over a high heat for about 5 minutes, until reduced by half. Transfer to a bowl, leave to cool, cover and refrigerate until well chilled. Whisk in the oil or red pepper juice, and season with salt and pepper to taste.

Put the chilled salad greens in a large serving bowl, and arrange the chrisophene on top. If the prawns are small, leave them whole; if they are medium-size, slice them through the centre lengthways; if large, slice them through the centre and then cut across, making each prawn into four pieces. Add the prawns to the salad and sprinkle with the capers. Pour the dressing over and serve garnished with sweet onion rings, if liked.

FRUIT CRAB SALAD

Serves 4

Ocean sticks or crab sticks work well in this salad because when served cold in a no-cook dish, the white-fish based dish is very similar to more expensive crabmeat. Of course, if you prefer to use real crabmeat, by all means do so. If using fresh pineapple, cut lengthways into quarters, cutting through crown, remove fruit from shells, discard core and reserve shells to use as 'pineapple boats'.

INGREDIENTS

1 large fresh pineapple, or 450-g/16-oz can unsweetened pineapple, cut into bite-sized chunks, drained

950 g/2 lb crabmeat, cut into chunks, or ocean sticks or crab sticks

1 large mango, peeled and cubed

225 g/8 oz orange-flesh melon balls

225 g/8 oz seedless grapes

yogurt or soured cream to serve (optional)

COMBINE PINEAPPLE, crabmeat or ocean sticks, mango, melon balls and grapes. Place in your pineapple boats or in a glass bowl. Chill until ready to serve. Serve with yogurt or soured cream, if desired.

Hawaiian Salad ▶

MEAT, POULTRY & GAME SALADS

COBB SALAD

Serves 4–6

There are many variations of this classic American layered salad, but it almost always includes Cos lettuce, chicken, a blue cheese, bacon and hard-boiled eggs. It is said to have been invented at Hollywood's Brown Derby restaurant.

INGREDIENTS

½ round lettuce, shredded

½ iceberg lettuce, shredded

½ bunch watercress, cleaned with tough stalks discarded

2 large tomatoes, diced

350–450 g/¾–1 lb cooked chicken breast, diced

2 avocados, peeled, stoned, and diced

1 large carrot, peeled and grated

4 rashes crisply cooked bacon, crumbled

2 tbsp chopped spring onions

100 g/4 oz Roquefort or Gorgonzola cheese, crumbled

2 hard-boiled eggs, finely chopped

10 stoned black olives, sliced

100 ml/4 fl oz French vinaigrette

LINE A SHALLOW salad bowl with the two types of lettuce and the watercress. Arrange the tomato, chicken and avocado in three separate strips across the bowl. Scatter the carrot and bacon over the salad. Add the spring onions and cheese, and then the eggs. Top with the olives. Drizzle with the dressing and serve immediately.

CHEF'S SALAD

Serves 4–6

This salad evolved mainly in American hotel restaurants. Today, it is a popular lunchtime salad. You can substitute beef tongue for the ham, if you prefer.

INGREDIENTS

½ tsp salt

30 ml/2 tbsp vinegar

90 ml/6 tbsp olive oil

freshly ground black pepper

½ iceberg lettuce, finely shredded

white part of 1 spring onion, finely chopped

225 g/8 oz cooked ham, cut into thin strips

225 g/8 oz cooked chicken or turkey, cut into thin strips

100 g/4 oz Swiss or Jarlsburg cheese cut into thin strips

1 tsp finely chopped fresh parsley

1 tsp finely chopped fresh basil

1 tsp finely chopped fresh tarragon

1 medium ripe tomato, cut into wedges, to garnish

WHISK TOGETHER THE salt, vinegar and olive oil. Season with pepper to taste. Put the lettuce and spring onion in a large bowl, pour over half the dressing, and toss. Line the bottom of a salad bowl with the dressed lettuce and spring onion, and arrange the strips of ham, chicken or turkey and cheese on top. Pour the remaining dressing over the salad, sprinkle on the herbs and garnish.

Cobb Salad ▶

MONTE CRISTO SALAD

Serves 4

This is named for the sandwich of ham, turkey and cheese served on French toast. Serve this salad with warm crostini, if desired, to follow through on the theme.

INGREDIENTS

15 ml/1 tbsp white wine vinegar

2 tsp Dijon mustard

¼ tsp dried red pepper flakes

⅛ tsp freshly ground black pepper

75 g/3 oz cooked lean ham, cut into thin strips

75 g/3 oz cooked turkey or chicken breast, cut into thin strips

40 g/1½ oz Jarlsberg or Muenster cheese, cut into thin strips

100 g/4 oz celery, chopped

50 g/2 oz carrots, grated

50 g/2 oz red onion, thinly sliced

2 tbsp chopped parsley

IN A LARGE bowl, whisk together the vinegar, mustard, pepper flakes and black pepper. Add the ham, turkey or chicken, cheese, celery, carrot, onion and parsley. Toss well to coat. Cover and refrigerate until thoroughly chilled. Stir well before serving.

FLORIDIAN KING GASPARILLA BEEF SALAD

Serves 4–6

This Floridian salad was created in honour of an annual festival, similar to Mardi Gras, which commemorates the days of pirates and is celebrated with floats, costumes and frivolity.

INGREDIENTS

1 large iceberg lettuce, shredded

2 celery stalks, finely chopped

25 g/1 oz salted, dry-roasted peanuts, finely chopped,

2 rashers crisply cooked bacon, crumbled

35 g/1¼ oz dried beef, finely shredded

25 g/1 oz carrot, chopped

100 g/4 oz low-fat blue cheese dressing

IN A LARGE bowl, combine the lettuce, celery, peanuts, bacon, beef and carrot, and mix well. Toss with the dressing and serve immediately.

◀ *Monte Cristo Salad*

DIJON BEEF STIR-FRY SALAD

Serves 4

Use your favourite Dijon-style mustard in this dish. I prefer the spicy varieties, but you may like the more mellow, honeyed ones. If you do not have any available, add some honey to any other style of mustard and omit the sugar in the recipe.

INGREDIENTS

15 ml/1 tbsp olive oil

450 g/1 lb fillet of beef, trimmed and cut into 4-cm/1½-inch pieces

salt and freshly ground black pepper

275 g/10 oz salad greens

PARMESAN CROUTONS

¼ loaf French or Italian bread

22.5 ml/1½ tbsp extra-virgin olive oil

1 garlic clove, crushed

15 g/½ oz grated Parmesan cheese

DRESSING

100 ml/4 fl oz olive oil

50 ml/2 fl oz Dijon mustard

50 ml/2 fl oz balsamic vinegar

1 garlic clove, crushed

1 tsp sugar

salt and freshly ground black pepper

MAKE THE DRESSING by whisking together the olive oil, mustard, vinegar, garlic, sugar and salt and pepper to taste in a medium bowl. Set aside.

In a large nonstick frying pan, heat the oil over medium-high heat. Add the beef, a few pieces at a time, and stir-fry for 2–3 minutes, or until browned. Season with a little salt and pepper, and set aside.

In a large bowl, combine the salad greens with half the dressing, tossing to coat.

Now make the croutons. Cut the crusts off the bread, then slice the bread into 1-cm/½-inch cubes. Heat the oil and garlic in a heavy frying pan over a medium heat for 5 minutes, or until the garlic is golden. Discard the garlic. Add the bread cubes and cook, stirring frequently, until lightly browned, 3–5 minutes. Leftover croutons can be stored in a tightly covered jar for up to 3 days. They should be lightly toasted on a baking sheet before using.

Arrange the salad greens on a serving platter, top with the cooked beef, and sprinkle with the croutons. Serve immediately, passing the remaining dressing separately.

STIR-FRY PORK AND VEGETABLE SALAD

Serves 4

The vegetables can be altered according to taste or availability.

INGREDIENTS

vegetable oil for frying

115 g/4 oz piece of pork loin, cut into fine strips

1 small turnip, cut into 5-cm/2-in long strips

1 small carrot, cut into 5-cm/2-in long strips

1 small onion, cut into 5-cm/2-in long strips

2–3 celery stalks, cut into 5-cm/2-in long strips

50 g/2 oz mushroom caps, cut into 5-cm/2-in long strips

1 small garlic clove, crushed and finely chopped

1 tsp grated fresh ginger root

2 spring onions, white and some green parts finely chopped

45 ml/3 tbsp soy sauce

7.5 ml/1½ tsp sesame oil

1 tbsp sugar

5 ml/1 tsp rice vinegar

freshly ground black pepper

sesame seeds for garnish

HEAT ABOUT 2 tablespoons of oil in a frying pan, add the pork, and stir-fry for 3–4 minutes until cooked through. Using a slotted spoon, remove it to a bowl.

Add the turnip and carrot strips to the pan and fry for 5–7 minutes until just beginning to soften.

Add the onion and celery to a saucepan of boiling water and simmer for 2–3 minutes. Drain and refresh under running cold water. Add to the pork with the mushrooms, garlic, ginger and spring onions.

Using a slotted spoon transfer the turnips and carrots to kitchen paper towels to drain.

Whisk together the soy sauce, sesame oil, sugar and rice vinegar. Add the turnips and carrots to the pork, pour over the dressing and toss. Leave until cold. Sprinkle with sesame seeds.

SOBA GRILLED BEEF SALAD

Serves 4–6

This salad, inspired by Japanese cuisine, can be made with leftover beef. Soba noodles are made
from wheat and can be found in many specialist and oriental food shops. If you cannot find them, you can substitute
linguine, but the result will not be quite as Japanese in style.

INGREDIENTS

225 g/8 oz soba noodles, broken into
bite-size pieces

225 g/8 oz trimmed grilled steak or
cooked roast beef, thinly sliced and cut
into strips

2 tomatoes, coarsely diced

I sweet white onion, peeled, halved
lengthways, thinly sliced crossways, and
separated into half-rings

15 g/½ oz chopped fresh parsley

15 g/½ oz chopped fresh basil

75 g/3 oz Cos or iceberg lettuce,
shredded

parsley and coriander sprigs, to garnish

DRESSING

50 ml/2 fl oz rice wine vinegar

2 tbsp mayonnaise

30 ml/2 tbsp extra virgin olive oil

½ tsp dried oregano

½ tsp ground cumin

I tsp salt

¼ tsp freshly ground black pepper

¼ tsp ground red chilli

MAKE THE DRESSING by whisking together the vinegar, mayonnaise and olive oil in a large bowl. Then whisk in the oregano, cumin, salt, black pepper and ground chilli until well blended. Set aside. Cook the soba noodles until *al dente*, according to the directions on the packet. Drain the noodles well, and add them to the dressing in the bowl. Toss in the beef, tomatoes, onion and herbs. Cover and refrigerate for 1–2 hours. Serve on a bed of lettuce, and garnish with parsley and coriander.

SPICY CHICKEN SALAD WITH MUSHROOMS

Serves 4

The subtle taste of mushrooms, the tang of oranges and the nutty taste of pecans complement
the spicy chicken in this salad.

INGREDIENTS

1 tsp salt

½ tsp cayenne pepper

½ tsp black pepper

¼ tsp fresh thyme

1 uncooked chicken breast,
skinned and cut into strips

30 ml/2 tbsp vegetable oil

275 g/10 oz torn lettuce or salad
greens

75 g/3 oz sliced mushrooms

50 g/2 oz pecans

2 satsuma oranges, segmented, or
1 × 300-g/11-oz can mandarin orange
segments

IN A SMALL bowl, mix the spices together. Toss the chicken in the spices, until chicken is well coated.

In a frying pan, heat the oil, sauté the chicken until brown all over. Drain well on kitchen paper towels and refrigerate the chicken until ready to serve.

In a salad bowl, toss the greens, mushrooms, pecans, oranges and chicken. Serve with a favourite dressing.

CAPERED DUCK SALAD

Serves 4

Substitute chicken breast if you do not want the excess calories of duck, which is one of the fattiest meats.
This recipe would also work quite well with leftover roast pork.

INGREDIENTS

400 g/14 oz skinned, boned, roasted duck, roughly shredded

175 g/6 oz boiled potatoes, peeled and cut into 1-cm/½-in cubes

50 g/2 oz dill pickles, diced

25 g/1 oz spring onions, chopped

2 tbsp diced red pepper

4 stoned black olives, sliced

75 ml/5 tbsp plus 10 ml/2 tsp non-fat or low-fat soured cream

15 ml/1 tbsp plus 5 ml/1 tsp non-fat or low-fat mayonnaise

1 tbsp chopped drained capers

2 tsp Dijon mustard

salt and freshly ground black pepper

IN A MEDIUM mixing bowl, combine the duck, potatoes, dill pickles, spring onions, pepper and olives. Set aside. In a small bowl, whisk together the soured cream, mayonnaise, capers and mustard. Season with salt and pepper to taste. Add to the salad just before serving, mixing gently to combine.

TROPICAL PORK SALAD WITH ORANGE-MINT DRESSING

Serves 4

Here's a marvellous way to use up leftover pork.
(You might just find yourself cooking pork so you can make this delicious salad!)

INGREDIENTS

1 tsp finely grated orange rind

50 ml/2 fl oz fresh orange juice

22.5 ml/1½ tbsp cider vinegar

2 tbsp chopped fresh mint leaves or 1 tbsp dried

¾ tsp French mustard

¼ tsp salt

¼ tsp freshly ground pepper

100 ml/4 fl oz olive oil

450 g/1 lb cooked pork, shredded

1 large ripe paw-paw (450 g/1 lb) peeled, halved, seeded, and cut into 1-cm/½-in chunks

1 ripe avocado (275 g/10oz) stoned, peeled, and cut into 1-cm/½-in chunks

1 small red onion, thinly sliced

150 g/5 oz lettuce, fresh spinach, or chicory torn into pieces

40 g/1½ oz slivered almonds, toasted

WHISK TOGETHER THE orange rind and juice, vinegar, mint, mustard, salt and pepper in a large bowl. Gradually whisk in the oil until blended. Gently stir in the pork, paw-paw, avocado and onion, tossing to mix and coat. Mound the salad on a serving dish lined with lettuce, spinach or chicory and sprinkle with almonds.

CHICKEN SALAD WITH CHERRIES AND TARRAGON

Serves 4–6

A rice salad makes a good accompaniment to this dish.

INGREDIENTS

150 ml/¼ pint real mayonnaise

75 ml/3 fl oz Greek yogurt

a good tbsp freshly chopped tarragon

freshly ground white pepper

pinch of salt

575 g/1¼ lb cooked chicken, diced

225 g/8 oz fresh cherries, pitted

extra tarragon leaves, to garnish

MIX THE MAYONNAISE in a bowl with the yogurt, chopped tarragon, pepper and salt. Leave for 30 minutes for the flavours to combine.

Add the chicken and stir so that the chicken is coated in the dressing. Stir in the cherries just before serving and garnish with the extra tarragon.

SPRINGTIME CHICKEN SALAD

Serves 4

Inspired by classic chicken salad, this variation marries the citrusy flavour and aroma of oranges with chicken and asparagus. Use reduced-sodium chicken stock, if you are concerned about salt intake.

INGREDIENTS

lettuce leaves

500 g/1¼ lb cooked chicken, skinned, boned, and sliced

450 g/1 lb cooked asparagus

2 oranges, peeled, segmented and seeded

DRESSING

10 ml/2 tsp olive oil

1 tsp curry powder

225 ml/8 fl oz chicken stock

75 ml/5 tbsp non-fat soured cream

30 ml/2 tbsp orange juice

10 ml/2 tsp honey

1 tsp grated orange rind

5 ml/1 tsp lemon juice

salt

FIRST PREPARE THE dressing. Heat the oil and curry powder in a small saucepan over a medium-low heat for about 4 minutes. Add the stock and simmer for about 15 minutes, until reduced to 75 ml/5 tbsp. Whisk in the soured cream, orange juice, honey, orange rind, lemon juice and salt to taste. Pour into a small heatproof jug, and refrigerate for about 2 hours.

After the dressing has chilled, arrange the lettuce leaves on four plates. Top with the chicken, asparagus and orange segments. Drizzle half the chilled dressing over the salad and pass the rest separately.

CORIANDER CHICKEN

Serves 4

A few simple ingredients make this impressively exotic salad.

INGREDIENTS

1.5 kg/3 lb chicken, cut into
5-cm/2-in pieces

1 tsp salt

½ tsp freshly ground black pepper

3 garlic cloves

10 ml/2 tsp lemon juice

2 tbsp ground coriander

1 small bunch fresh coriander

40 g/1½ oz butter or margarine

SEASON THE CHICKEN with the salt, pepper, garlic, lemon juice and half the ground coriander. Chop the fresh cilantro finely and mix it in with the chicken. Marinate for 4 hours.

Preheat the oven to 180°C/350°F/ Gas Mark 4. Drain the chicken. Melt the butter or margarine. Place the chicken in a heatproof dish, and pour the melted butter or margarine over the chicken. Sprinkle with the remaining ground coriander, then bake for 1 hour or until cooked.

Just before serving, grill the chicken to brown it. Serve with rice and salad.

FRIED CHICKEN SALAD

Serves 2

Make salad into a main dish with the addition of warm strips of fried chicken. For ease of cooking and slicing, use boneless chicken breasts. Top with a favorite buttermilk-style dressing.

INGREDIENTS
CHICKEN

40 g/1½ oz flour

¼ tsp salt

½ tsp paprika

¼ tsp black pepper

¼ tsp dried thyme

⅛ tsp celery salt

2 chicken breasts, boneless

oil for frying

SALAD

chicken strips

65–75 g/2½–3 oz lettuce leaves, any type, torn

50 g/2 oz mushrooms, sliced

1 celery stalk, diced

1 spring onion, chopped

stoned black olives

MIX FLOUR AND seasonings. Dredge chicken in seasoned flour. Heat 5 mm/¼ in oil in frying pan. When it's hot but not smoking, carefully add chicken. Fry over medium heat, turning once, until outside is crispy and no pink is visible when you cut into the chicken, 10–15 minutes, depending on thickness of the meat.

Let the chicken cool slightyl and cut into strips. Divide the lettuce, mushrooms, celery, spring onion and olives between two plates. Arrange chicken on top of salad.

Coriander Chicken ▶

HAM AND AVOCADO SALAD

Serves 4

The perfect light dish for a warm summer day.

INGREDIENTS

350 g/12 oz fresh pasta shapes
30 ml/2 tbsp cider vinegar
1 tsp prepared wholegrain mustard
½ tsp caster sugar
salt and freshly ground black pepper
90 ml/6 tbsp olive oil
450 g/1 lb lean cooked ham (in one piece), cubed

2 avocados
4 tbsp snipped chives
50 g/2 oz walnuts, chopped
1 lettuce heart or ½ iceberg lettuce, shredded (optional)

COOK THE PASTA in boiling salted water for 3 minutes, then drain well. Meanwhile, mix the cider vinegar, mustard, caster sugar, and seasoning in a basin. Whisk the mixture until the sugar and salt have dissolved. Gradually whisk in the oil. Place the hot pasta into a dish and pour the dressing over it, then mix well.

Allow the pasta to cool slightly before mixing in the ham. Just before serving the salad, halve the avocados, remove their stones and quarter the halves lengthways. Remove the peel, then cut the flesh into chunks and mix them with the pasta. Mix in the chives and walnuts.

Arrange the salad on a base of shredded lettuce, if liked, and serve promptly. If the salad is allowed to stand, the avocado will discolour.

FRANKFURTER SALAD

Serves 4

This salad is a good stand-by when unexpected guests arrive.

INGREDIENTS

225 g/8 oz fresh pasta shapes or small pasta squares
½ small onion, chopped
225 g/8 oz white cabbage, shredded
2 carrots, coarsely grated
150 ml/¼ pint mayonnaise

8 frankfurters, sliced
salt and freshly ground black pepper
25 g/1 oz chopped roasted peanuts

COOK THE PASTA in boiling salted water for 3 minutes, then drain it and allow to cool. Mix the onion, cabbage, carrots and mayonnaise. Toss the pasta and frankfurters with the cabbage mixture and seasoning. Divide between four serving bowls. Sprinkle with peanuts and serve at once, offering plenty of warmed crusty bread with the salad.

Ham and Avocado Salad ▶

MONGOLIAN BEEF SALAD

Serves 4–6

This salad has an oriental flavour, but the ingredients are all easily available. You can prepare the toasted sesame seeds and most of the other ingredients up to a day ahead.

INGREDIENTS

675 g/1½ lb broccoli

275 g/10 oz mushrooms, thinly sliced

2 spring onions, thinly sliced

1 small Cos lettuce

1 small yellow pepper, cut into long, thin strips

1 small red pepper, cut into long, thin strips

12 radishes, trimmed

450 g/1 lb thinly sliced, cooked roast beef

toasted sesame seeds, to garnish

DRESSING

50 ml/2 fl oz rapeseed or corn oil

50 ml/2 fl oz rice wine vinegar

30 ml/2 tbsp soy sauce

10 ml/2 tsp dark sesame oil

10 ml/¼ tsp garlic powder

¼ tsp freshly ground pepper

PLACE ALL THE dressing ingredients in a jar with a tight-fitting lid. Shake vigorously until well blended. Set aside at room temperature to let the flavours develop.

Bring about 25 cm/1 in of lightly salted water to the boil in a large pot. Add the broccoli, cover, and cook for 4–5 minutes, until crisp-tender. Drain in a colander and refresh under cold running water. Drain again, place in a plastic food bag or a lidded container, and refrigerate for 2–24 hours.

In a medium bowl, combine the mushrooms and spring onions with 30 ml/2 tbsp of the dressing. Toss to coat evenly, then place in a sealed plastic bag or a lidded container, and refrigerate for 2–24 hours.

Refrigerate the remaining dressing.

Remove 12 small leaves from the lettuce, and pack them, along with the peppers and radishes, in food bags or storage containers. Refrigerate for 2–24 hours

To serve, line a large platter with lettuce leaves. Roll up the roast beef slices and arrange them in centre of the platter. Spoon the mushroom mixture on to the platter, next to the meat. Arrange the broccoli and pepper strips on the other side of the meat, and drizzle with 30 ml/2 tbsp of the reserved dressing. Scatter radishes around the platter. Drizzle the remaining dressing over the salad, sprinkle toasted sesame seeds on top, and serve.

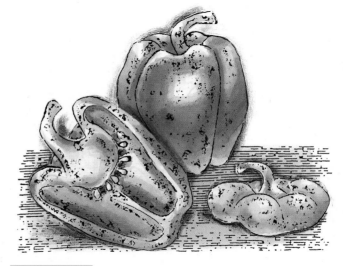

PURA VIDA TACO SALAD

Serves 4–6

Instead of using packaged tortilla chips in this recipe, you may like to use soft flour or corn tortillas, baked in a hot oven until they are golden and crispy. You could also substitute low-fat or non-fat soured cream to further reduce the calories in this salad, whose name means 'healthy natural life'.

INGREDIENTS

225 g/8 oz minced beef or turkey, cooked, crumbled and drained

2 tbsp finely chopped canned mild green chillies

½ × 400-g/14-oz can whole peeled tomatoes, undrained

1 tsp chilli powder

1 tsp garlic salt

freshly ground black pepper

1 Cos lettuce, roughly chopped

90 g/3½ oz tortilla chips or corn chips

50 g/2 oz Cheddar cheese, grated

100 g/4 oz spring onions with green tops, chopped

½ medium tomato, coarsely chopped

12 black olives, sliced

soured cream

sliced spring onions, to garnish (optional)

2 pickled red chillies, to garnish

COMBINE THE MINCED beef or turkey, chillies, whole tomatoes, chillie powder, garlic salt and pepper to taste in a frying pan. Mix well with a large wooden spoon and cook over low heat, uncovered, for about 30 minutes, or until most of the moisture has evaporated. Cover and set aside.

Place the lettuce in a large chilled bowl and arrange tortilla chips around the outer edge. Top with the meat mixture and sprinkle cheese, spring onions, chopped tomato and sliced olives around the meat. Top with a spoonful of soured cream garnished with spring onions and the pickled red chillies. Serve immediately.

MAJ-JONG CLUB CHICKEN SALAD

Serves 4

The Chinese flair for combining a variety of textures and tastes comes together in
this delightful salad. Serve with some sticky rice or a hot-and-sour soup, and garnish with greens and
cherry tomatoes, and you have a complete Chinese-style dinner.

INGREDIENTS

2 medium carrots, thinly sliced

225 g/8 oz mangetout

30 ml/2 tbsp vegetable oil

30 ml/2 tbsp lemon juice

5 ml/1 tsp soy sauce

2.5 ml/½ tsp sesame oil

¼ tsp ground ginger

about 350–450 g/¾ lb cooked chicken
breast, cubed

1 x 225-g/8-oz can water chestnuts

4 spring onions, thinly sliced

COOK CARROTS IN a saucepan of
boiling water for about 5
minutes. Add mangetout and cook
1 minute more, or until the vegetables
are crisp-tender. Drain and set aside.

Whisk the vegetable oil, lemon
juice, soy sauce, sesame oil and ginger
in a serving bowl. Add the chicken,
water chestnuts, spring onions and the
cooked carrots and mangetout to the
bowl. Mix well to coat evenly. Serve at
room temperature, or refrigerate for
up to 1 hour before serving.

SPICY BLACK BEAN AND HAM HOCK SALAD

Serves 4

This tastes best made from scratch, but if you're in a hurry, here's a no-cook version: simply substitute
2 x 450-g/1-lb cans beans, drained and rinsed, and stir in ground versions of the spices and any minced cooked ham or
pork. Whip up the vinaigrette in the same manner as below.

INGREDIENTS

225 g/8 oz black beans

2 large ham hocks

1 large bay leaf

1 tsp coriander seeds, cracked

1 tsp cumin seeds, crushed

1 tsp red chilli pepper flakes

¼ tsp ground cinnamon

50 ml/2 fl oz lime juice

15 ml/1 tbsp sherry vinegar

1 tsp ground cumin

15 ml/1 tbsp olive oil

15 ml/1 tbsp Tabasco or other hot pepper sauce

1 garlic clove, crushed

2 tbsp finely chopped red pepper

2 tbsp finely chopped spring onion

salt and freshly ground black pepper

25 g/1 oz fresh coriander stems removed, rinsed and dried

SOAK THE BEANS, if necessary, according to the directions on the packet. Place the beans in a large heavy-based saucepan. Add the ham hocks, bay leaf, coriander seeds, cumin seeds, chilli flakes and cinnamon. Add fresh cold water to cover. Simmer gently over medium heat until the beans are tender, about 45 minutes. Remove the ham hocks and set aside to cool. Remove the bay leaf and discard. Drain the beans and rinse under cold running water until chilled. Set aside.

Combine the lime juice and sherry vinegar in a nonreactive bowl. Whisk in the ground cumin, olive oil, Tabasco and garlic. Stir in the red pepper, spring onion and salt and pepper to taste. Set aside.

Pull the ham off the hock, discarding the bone and fat. Mince the meat and place it in a salad bowl. Add the beans and coriander. Pour the vinaigrette over the mixture and toss to combine. Season to taste with salt, pepper and additional Tabasco.

GRAIN, BEAN & PASTA SALADS

TEX-MEX CORN AND BLACK BEAN SALAD

Serves 6–8

This healthy salad has only the smallest amount of oil in it, with the juice from the corn
used as a substitute for part of the oil. Unlike some other Tex-Mex bean dishes, this one does not depend on fat for
flavour, and it is nutritious and low in calories.

INGREDIENTS

1 × 350-g/12-oz can sweetcorn kernels, drained with juice reserved

1 × 425-g/15-oz can black beans, drained and rinsed

1 red pepper, finely chopped

50 g/2 oz spring onions, chopped

50 g/2 oz red onion, chopped

1 garlic clove, finely chopped

1 medium tomato, chopped

1 jalapeño chilli, seeded and finely chopped (optional)

coriander sprigs or red onion wedges, to garnish

DRESSING

50 ml/2 fl oz corn juice, measured out from the reserved juice

50 ml/2 fl oz red wine vinegar

50 ml/2 fl oz olive oil

1.25 ml/¾ tsp hot pepper sauce

½ tsp chilli powder

15 ml/1 tbsp fresh lemon or lime juice

1 tbsp chopped fresh coriander

IN A LARGE bowl, combine the corn, beans, pepper, spring onions, red onion, garlic, tomato and jalapeño. Set aside.

To make the dressing, place the corn juice, vinegar, olive oil, hot pepper sauce, chilli powder, lemon or lime juice and coriander in a jar with a tight-fitting lid. Tighten the lid and shake to mix well. Pour the dressing over the salad and stir to mix. Cover and refrigerate for at least 6 hours, or overnight. To serve, transfer the salad to an attractive bowl and garnish with a few sprigs of coriander or thin wedges of red onion.

OLD CALIFORNIA INN RICE SALAD

Serves 4

This salad is adapted from a recipe served at an old stagecoach stop in California in the Santa Ynez valley, northwest of Santa Barbara.

INGREDIENTS

300 ml/½ pint chicken stock

90 g/3½ oz long-grain white rice, uncooked

1 x 175-g/6-oz jar artichoke hearts

2 spring onions, chopped

25 g/1 oz pimento-stuffed green olives, sliced

½ medium green pepper, diced

1 celery stalk, diced

1 tbsp chopped fresh parsley

¼ tsp curry powder

¼ cup mayonnaise

salt and freshly ground black pepper

BRING THE CHICKEN stock to the boil in a large saucepan. Add the long-grain white rice and return to boiling point. Reduce heat, cover and simmer for 20 minutes, or until all the liquid is absorbed. Transfer the rice to a large serving bowl and leave to cool.

Drain the artichoke hearts thoroughly, reserving the liquid for the dressing.

Chop the artichoke hearts. Add the artichokes, spring onions, olives, green pepper, celery and parsley to the cooled rice. To make the dressing, mix together the reserved artichoke liquid, curry powder and mayonnaise in a small bowl. Season with salt and pepper to taste. Pour the dressing over the rice salad and mix well to combine. Refrigerate before serving.

TOMATO RICE SALAD

Serves 4

This is a popular Portuguese rice dish. Much of its character comes from the well-flavoured, locally grown tomatoes. Serve the rice with roast, grilled or fried meat, poultry and fish, fish cakes and omelettes.

INGREDIENTS

30 ml/2 tbsp olive oil

1 large onion, finely chopped

1 garlic clove, finely chopped

2 ripe, well-flavoured tomatoes, skinned, seeded and finely chopped

225 g/8 oz long-grain white rice

boiling water

2 tbsp chopped parsley

salt and pepper

HEAT THE OIL in a saucepan, add the onion and garlic, and fry until softened but not brown.

Stir in the tomatoes, cook for a further 5 minutes or so before adding the rice. Stir to coat with the vegetables; then add boiling water to 2½ times the volume of the rice. Bring to the boil, cover and cook over a low heat until the rice is tender and all the liquid has been absorbed. Stir in the parsley and seasoning to taste.

◀ *Old California Inn Rice Salad*

THREE-BEAN SALAD IN A CORIANDER DRESSING

Serves 4–6

This salad takes a little time to make, but the flavour is so much more robust than canned
three-bean salads that it is worth the trouble. You may want to double the recipe, so you can serve it again.
The salad will keep, covered, in the refrigerator for about one week.

INGREDIENTS

225 g/8 oz dried black beans, rinsed

225 g/8 oz dried white beans, rinsed

1 garlic clove

1 bottle of pickled jalapeño chillies,
drained and with chillies seeded,
if desired

25 g/1 oz fresh coriander leaves

50 ml/2 fl oz fresh lemon juice

100 ml/4 fl oz plus 15 ml/1 tbsp
rapeseed or vegetable oil

salt

225 g/8 oz green beans, trimmed and
cut into 2.5-cm/1-in pieces

PLACE THE BLACK beans in a large saucepan, and add triple their volume of cold water. In another large saucepan, place the white beans with the same proportion of cold water. Bring the water to the boil in both pans and simmer the beans, uncovered, for 2 minutes. Remove the pans from the heat, and leave the beans to soak for 1 hour. Drain each pan of beans separately through a colander. Refill each pan with 1.15 L/ 2 pints water. Stir the black beans into the water in one pan, and the white beans into the water in the other. Cook the beans at a low simmer, testing for tenderness every 5 minutes for 15–40 minutes: they are cooked when they are just tender but still hold their shape. Drain the beans and leave them to cool slightly.

In a blender, purée half a garlic clove, the chillies and half the coriander with half the lemon juice, 100 ml/4 fl oz of the oil and salt to taste, scraping down the side of the blender, until the dressing is completely smooth. Transfer the cooked beans to a very large bowl, and toss with the dressing. Cover, refrigerate and leave to marinate overnight, stirring occasionally.

The next day, boil the green beans in a saucepan of boiling, salted water for 5 minutes, or until they are crisp-tender. Drain, refresh under cold water, and pat them dry. In a blender, purée the remaining half a garlic clove with the remaining coriander and oil, adding salt to taste and scraping down the side of the blender until the dressing is smooth. Add the green beans and the dressing to the bowl of dressed beans, toss the salad well, and serve it at room temperature.

CHICK PEA AND CHERRY TOMATO SALAD

Serves 4

This recipe is inspired by Indian salads, but uses ingredients that are readily available. The salad makes a wonderful accompaniment for Indian or Mediterranean dishes.

INGREDIENTS

1 garlic clove, lightly crushed

30 ml/2 tbsp olive oil

15 ml/1 tbsp lemon juice

⅛ tsp salt

⅛ tsp pepper

1 × 450-g/16-oz can chick peas, drained and rinsed

225 g/8 oz halved cherry tomatoes

25 g/1 oz spring onions, finely chopped

lettuce leaves, to serve (optional)

RUB THE INSIDE of a medium serving bowl with the crushed garlic. Discard the garlic. Whisk the oil, lemon juice, salt and pepper in the bowl. Add the chick peas, tomatoes and spring onions. Cover and refrigerate for up to 24 hours, stirring occasionally. Serve on a bed of lettuce, if desired.

CALDO GALLEGO SALAD

Serves 4

This salad is inspired by the famous Galician soup of Spain, a dish that is also popular with Cubans and other Spanish-speaking groups of the Americas and Caribbean. The combination of velvety cannellini beans and ham works just as well in a salad as in a soup.

INGREDIENTS

1 carrot, peeled and thinly sliced

30 ml/2 tbsp olive oil

30 ml/2 tbsp lemon juice

¾ tsp ground dried sage

⅛ tsp pepper

1 × 450-g/15-oz can cannellini beans, drained and rinsed

100 g/4 oz ham, cut into 5-mm/¼-in cubes

1 celery stalk, thinly sliced

25 g/1 oz red onion, chopped

lettuce leaves, to serve (optional)

BOIL THE CARROT for 3–5 minutes, until lightly cooked. Drain and set aside. Whisk the oil, lemon juice, sage and pepper together in a medium bowl. Add the cooked carrot, beans, ham, celery and onion. Refrigerate for up to 1 hour before serving, if desired, and serve on a bed of lettuce.

RICE WITH PRAWNS AND TOMATOES

Serves 4

INGREDIENTS

30 ml/2 tbsp olive oil

1 garlic clove, crushed

2 tomatoes, peeled and chopped

1 tsp saffron

2 tsp salt

1 tsp paprika

225 g/8 oz peas

350 g/12 oz uncooked rice

freshly ground black pepper

600 ml/1 pint water

8 prawns,
cooked, shelled and deveined

12 scampi,
cooked, shelled and deveined

HEAT THE OIL in a saucepan, then fry the garlic in it for 2 minutes. Add the tomatoes, saffron, salt, paprika, peas, rice and freshly ground black pepper and fry for 5 minutes, then add the water.

Add the prawns and scampi and cook for 15 more minutes, or until the rice has cooked (if necessary adding some more water). Serve immediately.

Serve with a cucumber salad.

CORN SALAD

Serves 6

Marinated and served cold, this salad is a great way to use up any leftover vegetable in your refrigerator.

INGREDIENTS

450 g/1 lb corn kernels (7–8 fresh ears)

50 g/2 oz carrot, thinly sliced

50 g/2 oz courgette, thinly sliced

12 cherry tomatoes, halved

1 green pepper, chopped

½ small red onion, thinly sliced

75-g/3-oz can ripe olives, drained

1 tbsp capers

DRESSING

90 ml/6 tbsp olive oil

45 ml/3 tbsp white wine vinegar

5 ml/1 tsp fresh lemon juice

1 tsp Dijon mustard

1 tbsp fresh tarragon

½ tsp salt

¼ tsp black pepper

large pinch cayenne pepper

COOK CORN IN boiling water until tender, about 3 minutes, then drain. Rinse with cold water and drain again. Mix with all the salad ingredients in a bowl.

In a bottle or small bowl, mix together all the dressing ingredients. Shake or whisk to mix thoroughly. Pour over salad and stir to coat. Refrigerate several hours.

Rice with Prawns and Tomatoes ▶

LUCKY BLACK-EYED PEA SALAD

Serves 8

Black-eyed peas are not really peas, but beans. This salad is based on a Southern American dish, a region where eating black-eyed peas is considered good luck. You can buy them at most markets selling Caribbean produce.

INGREDIENTS

225 g/8 oz large macaroni

675 g/1½ lb canned black-eyed peas, drained

1 medium red pepper, chopped

1 medium green pepper, chopped

1 medium purple onion, chopped

175 g/6 oz sliced provolone cheese, cut into strips

75 g/3 oz sliced pepperoni, cut into strips

1 x 50-g/2-oz jar diced pimiento, drained

1 x 115-g/4½-oz jar sliced mushrooms

2 tbsp chopped fresh parsley

DRESSING

1 x 20-g/¾-oz packet Italian salad dressing mix, or a mixture of 2 tsp onion powder, 2 tsp garlic salt, 2 tsp ground oregano, ½ tsp ground thyme and ½ tsp sweet, mild paprika

¼ tsp pepper

50 g/2 oz sugar

100 ml/4 fl oz white wine vinegar

50 ml/2 fl oz rapeseed oil

COOK THE MACARONI according to manufacturers' instructions. Drain well, and transfer to a large serving bowl. Set aside. Combine black-eyed peas, macaroni, peppers, onion, cheese, pepperoni, pimiento, mushrooms and parsley in a large bowl. Mix well and set aside.

Place all the dressing ingredients in a jar with a tightly fitting lid. Cover and shake until ingredients are combined. Pour the dressing over the salad, mix gently, cover and refrigerate for at least 2 hours before serving.

MOROCCAN COUSCOUS SALAD

Serves 4

This aromatic salad is influenced by the cuisine of Morocco, where couscous is a staple food. These individual salads served in scooped-out, ripe tomatoes make a pretty party dish.

INGREDIENTS

4 medium tomatoes

350 g/12 oz couscous, cooked according to manufacturers instructions, and cooled

15 g/½ oz fresh basil, chopped

2 tbsp chopped fresh parsley

1 tbsp grated Parmesan cheese

1 tbsp sunflower seeds

10 ml/2 tsp balsamic vinegar

CUT OFF AND discard the tops of the tomatoes; scoop out the flesh without breaking the tomato shells. Chop the tomato flesh and place it in a large bowl. Add couscous, basil, parsley, cheese, sunflower seeds and vinegar, tossing to mix well. Spoon the mixture evenly into the tomato shells. Refrigerate for at least 1 hour, or overnight, before serving.

Lucky Black-eyed Pea Salad ▶

HERBY MUSHROOM PASTA SALAD

Serves 4–8

Any small pasta shapes would be suitable for this dish. It can be served as a filling main course at lunchtime,
or as an accompaniment.

INGREDIENTS

450 g/1 lb dried pasta shapes

dash of olive oil

225 g/8 oz cup mushrooms, quartered

1 red pepper, seeded and cut
into 1-cm/½-in squares

1 yellow pepper, seeded and
cut into 1-cm/½-in squares

100 g/4 oz stoned black olives

4 tbsp chopped fresh basil

2 tbsp chopped fresh parsley

DRESSING

10 ml/2 tsp red wine vinegar

1 tsp salt

freshly ground black pepper

60 ml/4 tbsp extra virgin olive oil

1 clove of garlic, crushed

1–2 tsp Dijon mustard

BRING A LARGE saucepan of water to the boil, and add the pasta shapes with a dash of olive oil. Cook for about 10 minutes, stirring occasionally, until tender. Drain and rinse under cold running water. Drain well again.

Place the cooked pasta shapes in a large salad bowl, and add the remaining salad ingredients. Mix together well to combine.

To make the dressing, place all the ingredients in a screw-top jar and shake well. Pour the dressing over the salad and toss together.

Cover and refrigerate for at least 30 minutes, then toss again to mix before serving.

EASTERN PASTA SALAD

Serves 4–6

A traditional combination of mint and lemon makes this dish a salad for summer. Choose your favourite pasta shapes for this recipe, and serve with warm pitta bread to mop up the delicious dressing.

INGREDIENTS

350 g/12 oz dried pasta

dash of olive oil

400-g/14-oz can chickpeas, drained

4 tbsp chopped, fresh mint

finely grated zest of 1 lemon

DRESSING

3 cloves of garlic, crushed

90 ml/6 tbsp extra virgin olive oil

45 ml/3 tbsp white wine vinegar

freshly squeezed juice of 1 lemon

salt and freshly ground black pepper

Bring a large saucepan of water to the boil, and add the pasta with a dash of olive oil. Cook for about 10 minutes, stirring occasionally, until tender. Drain and rinse under cold running water. Drain again and place in a large mixing bowl.

Add the chickpeas, mint and lemon zest to the pasta. Place all the dressing ingredients in a screw-top jar, and shake well to mix. Pour the dressing over the chickpea mixture and mix well to combine. Cover and chill for at least 30 minutes. Toss before serving.

WARM PASTA SALAD

Serves 4

This salad combines the saltiness of green olives, the crunch of walnuts and the goodness of fresh vegetables. Use freshly grated Parmesan cheese, not the packaged kind; you'll notice a big difference in flavour. The flavours are enhanced when this salad is served warm, but if you have any cold leftovers, add a splash of vinaigrette for flavour.

INGREDIENTS

225 g/8 oz fusilli or other pasta

6 asparagus stalks

45 ml/3 tbsp extra virgin olive oil

40 g/1½ oz fresh grated Parmesan, cheese, plus extra for topping

½ small courgette, thinly sliced

2 spring onions, chopped

50 g/2 oz walnut pieces

50 g/2 oz green olives, quartered

salt and pepper to taste

Cook pasta according to directions on packet. While the pasta is cooking, blanch the asparagus for 2–3 minutes in boiling water. Drain, then cut into 2.5-cm/1-in pieces.

When the pasta is cooked, drain but do not rinse, then put it in a large mixing bowl. Pour olive oil over pasta and toss with two forks. Add the Parmesan and toss again. Stir in the asparagus, courgettes, spring onions, walnuts and green olives. Add salt and pepper to taste. Serve with a sprinkling of Parmesan over the top.

TOMATO AND PASTA SALAD

Serves 6–8

Orecchiette are small, ear-shaped pasta. If they are not available, gnocchi pasta shapes (dumplings) will work just as well.

INGREDIENTS

550 g/1¼ lb fresh orecchiette

dash of olive oil

450 g/1 lb red and yellow tomatoes, chopped

15-cm/6-in piece cucumber, chopped

175 g/6 oz feta cheese, chopped

5 tbsp chopped fresh coriander

2 tbsp chopped fresh basil

cherry tomatoes and fresh coriander sprigs, to garnish

DRESSING

15 ml/1 tbsp white wine vinegar

60 ml/4 tbsp olive oil

2 cloves of garlic, crushed

salt and freshly ground black pepper

Bring a large saucepan of water to the boil, and add the orecchiette with a dash of olive oil. Cook for about 5 minutes, stirring occasionally, until tender. Drain and rinse under cold running water. Drain again and set aside.

Place the orecchiette in a large mixing bowl, and add the remaining salad ingredients. Mix to combine. To make the dressing, place all the ingredients in a screw-top jar and shake well. Pour the dressing over the salad, and toss to coat. Serve garnished with cherry tomatoes and coriander sprigs.

STORE-CUPBOARD SALAD

Serves 4–6

Use tiny pasta shapes for this salad and serve with warm, crusty French bread.

INGREDIENTS

100 g/4 oz dried pastina (tiny shapes)

dash of olive oil

400-g/14-oz can mixed beans, such as kidney, cannellini, flageolet, etc, drained

1 red pepper, seeded and very finely diced

2 tsp dried oregano

DRESSING

2 cloves of garlic, crushed

60 ml/4 tbsp extra virgin olive oil

30–40 ml/2–3 tbsp balsamic vinegar

1 tsp tomato purée

salt and freshly ground black pepper

Bring a large saucepan of water to the boil, and add the pastina with a dash of olive oil. Cook for about 8 minutes, stirring occasionally, until tender. Drain and rinse under cold running water. Drain again and place in a large mixing bowl.

Add the beans, red pepper and oregano to the pasta. Place all the dressing ingredients in a screw-top jar, and shake well to combine. Pour the dressing over the salad, toss and chill for at least 30 minutes before serving.

◀ *Tomato and Pasta Salad*

SMOKED SALMON AND PASTA COCKTAILS

Serves 4

This turns a comparatively small quantity of smoked salmon into an attractive starter.

INGREDIENTS

100 g/4 oz fresh fusilli

60 ml/4 tbsp mayonnaise

60 ml/4 tbsp soured cream

2 tbsp snipped chives

salt and freshly ground black pepper

4 endive leaves, roughly shredded

175 g/6 oz smoked salmon, shredded

2 tbsp chopped fresh dill

grated rind of ½ lemon

fresh dill sprigs, to garnish

4 lemon wedges, to serve

COOK THE PASTA in boiling salted water for 3 minutes. Drain and cool. Mix the mayonnaise, soured cream and chives with the pasta. Add seasoning to taste.

Arrange the endive in four glass dishes, then divide the pasta between the dishes. Mix the smoked salmon with the dill and lemon rind, then arrange the shreds on top of the pasta. Garnish with dill sprigs. Serve lemon wedges with the cocktails so that their juice may be sprinkled over the smoked salmon.

BEAN SPROUT AND RICE SALAD

Serves 4

This wholesome salad is delicious and easy to prepare.

INGREDIENTS

175-g/6-oz can bean sprouts

15 ml/1 tbsp vegetable oil

15 ml/1 tbsp soy sauce

1 small piece of ginger root, finely chopped

salt and freshly ground black pepper

6 spring onions

100 g/4 oz cooked long-grain rice

60 ml/4 tbsp salad oil

30 ml/2 tbsp lemon juice

½ tsp sugar

4 slices of Chinese leaves

DRAIN THE CAN of bean sprouts. Heat the vegetable oil in a small saucepan. Toss in the bean sprouts with the soy sauce and finely chopped ginger. Stir well. Cover and cook for 3 minutes on a low heat.

Turn the bean sprouts into a bowl and allow to cool. Season well. Chop the spring onions into small pieces and add to the cooled shoots. Retain a few pieces for garnish. Stir in the rice.

Mix the salad oil with the lemon juice in a screw-top jar. Arrange the Chinese leaves in the bottom of the salad bowl. Shake the oil and lemon juice dressing and pour over the bean shoots and rice. Mix well and arrange in the salad bowl. Garnish with a few rings of chopped spring onions.

Smoked Salmon and Pasta Cocktails ▶

SPAGHETTI AND SALAMI SALAD

Serves 4

This salad has a distinctly Mediterranean flavour. Choose only the best ingredients from the delicatessen.

INGREDIENTS

350 g/12 oz fresh spaghetti
4 tbsp pine nuts
175 g/6 oz salami, cut in strips
50 g/2 oz black olives, sliced
425-g/15-oz can artichoke hearts, drained
60 ml/2 tbsp cider vinegar
salt and freshly ground black pepper
½ tsp caster sugar
90 ml/6 tbsp olive oil
4 tbsp chopped parsley

CUT THE SPAGHETTI into 5 cm/2-in lengths, then cook it in boiling salted water for 3 minutes. Drain the pasta well in a fine sieve before tipping it into a bowl; leave to cool.

Roast the pine nuts in a small, dry, heavy-bottomed saucepan until they are lightly browned, then tip them over the pasta. Add the salami, olives and artichoke hearts. Mix the cider vinegar, seasoning and caster sugar in a screw-top jar. Shake well until the sugar dissolves, then add the olive oil and shake again.

Pour the dressing over the salad and mix well. Toss the parsley in after the dressing, immediately before serving the salad.

CRAB AND COURGETTE SALAD

Serves 4

This recipe is ideal for a light lunch or supper.

INGREDIENTS

225 g/8 oz fresh pasta shapes
225 g/8 oz small, young courgettes
6 spring onions, chopped
6 basil sprigs
salt and freshly ground black pepper
30 ml/2 tbsp lemon juice
30 ml/2 tbsp olive oil
175 g/6 oz crabmeat
4 hard-boiled eggs
4 tbsp chopped parsley

COOK THE PASTA in boiling salted water for 3 minutes. Drain well and place in a bowl. Trim and coarsely grate the courgettes, then add them to the pasta with the spring onions. Use scissors to shred the basil leaves and soft stem ends into the salad.

Seasoning to taste and mix in the lemon juice. Add the olive oil and mix well. Arrange the mixture in a serving dish, leaving a hollow in the middle.

Flake the crabmeat. Chop the eggs and mix them with the crab. Fork in the parsley and seasoning to taste, then spoon the mixture in the middle of the pasta. Serve at once; if the salad is allowed to stand, the pasta and courgettes become watery.

Spaghetti and Salami Salad ▶

SMOKED MACKEREL SALAD

Serves 4

This is simple, extremely well flavoured and delicious for a summer lunch. Serve crusty bread to complement the pasta.

INGREDIENTS

225 g/8 oz fresh pasta shapes

50 g/2 oz butter

50 g/2 oz fresh white breadcrumbs

grated rind of 1 lemon

4 tbsp chopped parsley

150 ml/¼ pint soured cream

60 ml/4 tbsp horseradish sauce

1 tsp finely chopped rosemary

4 spring onions, chopped

salt and freshly ground black pepper

4 smoked mackerel fillets, skinned and coarsely flaked

2 tomatoes, peeled and chopped

COOK THE PASTA in boiling salted water for 3 minutes, then drain it and set it aside to cool. Melt the butter in a frying pan, add the breadcrumbs, and fry them, stirring often, until they are crisp and golden. Remove from the heat, stir in the lemon rind and 2 tablespoons of the parsley, and leave to cool.

Mix the soured cream, horseradish sauce, rosemary and spring onions with the pasta. Toss the shapes well to coat them in the sauce, then add seasoning to taste. Lightly fork the smoked mackerel and remaining parsley into the pasta mixture, then spoon the salad into a shallow dish. Garnish with a neat line of chopped tomato and a couple of lines of the fried breadcrumb mixture. Serve promptly after garnishing so that the breadcrumbs are still crisp when eaten.

BLACK BEANS AND RICE SALAD

Serves 4–6

If you have some leftover cooked rice on hand, this dish can be whipped up in just a few minutes. It makes a filling, nutritious accompaniment to any light main dish.

INGREDIENTS

550 g/1¼ lb cooked or canned black beans, rinsed and drained

350 g/12 oz cooked rice

50 g/2 oz fresh coriander

50 ml/2 fl oz lime juice

175 ml/6 fl oz oil

50 g/2 oz chopped onion

2 cloves garlic, crushed

salt and freshly ground black pepper

pimiento or red pepper strips, to garnish (optional)

MIX THE BEANS, rice and coriander together in a bowl. Place the lime juice in a small bowl and whisk in the oil. Add the onion and garlic and toss with the beans. Add salt and pepper to taste and garnish with pimiento or red pepper. Serve at room temperature or chilled.

◀ *Smoked Mackerel Salad*

Mama Mia's Pasta Salad

Serves 4

While full of Italian ingredients, this pasta salad, like most pasta salads, is American. Italians prefer their noodles warm, but Americans have been eating the cold ones since the macaroni salad was created in the early 1900s. This is a great salad to make the day after you have a party, because you can embellish the salad with leftover cold cuts, such as hard salami, pastrami or ham.

INGREDIENTS

450 g/1lb dried pasta shapes, such as rotini, penne, fusilli or conchiglie

about 25 g/1 oz sun-dried tomatoes, soaked in hot water for 5 minutes, then drained

225 g/8 oz smoked mozzarella, cut into 1-cm/½-in cubes

1 x 450-g/1-lb can chickpeas, drained and rinsed

10–20 small strips of bottled pepperoncini

½ tsp dried red pepper flakes

25 g/1 oz fresh, flat-leaf parsley leaves

DRESSING

2 garlic cloves

1 tbsp Dijon mustard

75 ml/5 tbsp red wine vinegar

30 ml/2 tbsp balsamic vinegar

15 ml/1 tbsp water

100 ml/4 fl oz olive oil, or 100 ml/4 fl oz of juice extracted from red peppers with 10 ml/2 tsp of vegetable oil added

salt

COOK THE PASTA in a large pan of boiling salted water until *al dente*, then rinse under cold running water and drain well. Transfer the pasta to a very large bowl.

Make the dressing by combining the garlic, mustard, vinegars, water and oil in a blender or food processor, and blending until smooth. Add salt to taste. Pour the dressing over the pasta and toss to coat evenly. Stir in the sun-dried tomatoes, mozzarella, chickpeas, pepperoncini, red pepper flakes and parsley. Cover and refrigerate for 4 hours; make sure the mixture is thoroughly chilled before serving.

CAPONATA RICE SALAD

Serves 4–6

This recipe combines caponata, a popular relish in Italian restaurants, with Italian arborio rice, a risotto rice.
The rice makes the salad extra special because it is from the Piedmont, along the valley of the Po River, one of Italy's most
important rice-growing regions. If you have difficulty locating arborio rice, long-grain white rice may be substituted.

INGREDIENTS

I tbsp salt

300 g/11 oz arborio rice

I medium onion, cut into 5-mm/¼-in dice

90 ml/6 tbsp olive oil

I small aubergine, cut into 1-cm/½-in dice

2 garlic cloves, finely chopped

45 ml/3 tbsp balsamic vinegar

3 large ripe tomatoes, seeded and cut into 1-cm/½-in dice

2 tbsp drained capers

25 g/1 oz stoned green olives, coarsely chopped

15 g/½ oz finely chopped mixed fresh herbs, such as basil, marjoram, mint, oregano and parsley

salt and freshly ground black pepper

BRING 2.25 L/4 PINTS of water to the boil in a large saucepan. Stir in the salt. Add the rice and cook, uncovered, over a moderate heat for about 12 minutes, until *al dente*. Drain, rinse with cold water, and drain again. Set aside.

While the rice is cooking, sauté the onion with 30 ml/2 tbsp of the oil in a large frying pan over a moderately high heat. Cook for about 5 minutes, until the onion becomes translucent. Add the aubergine, garlic and another 15 ml/1 tbsp of the oil, and cook for about 7 minutes, until the aubergine is soft.

Transfer the rice to a large bowl and toss with the remaining 45 ml/3 tbsp olive oil and the balsamic vinegar. Add the cooked aubergine mixture, tomatoes, capers, olives and fresh herbs, tossing to mix well. Season with salt and pepper to taste. Leave to stand for at least 20 minutes before serving.

SPICED RICE SALAD

Serves 4

Garam masala adds "warmth" to this tasty dish.

INGREDIENTS

225 g/8 oz rice

I tsp salt

I tsp garam masala

I tsp turmeric

I bay leaf

25 g/1 oz butter

I garlic clove, crushed

I onion, peeled and diced

50 g/2 oz sultanas

I green pepper, seeded, blanched and diced

90 ml/6 tbsp low-fat yogurt

2 spring onions, washed

COOK THE RICE in boiling salted water with the garam masala, turmeric and bay leaf for about 15 minutes until tender. Meanwhile melt the butter and gently sweat the garlic and onion without browning for 5 minutes. Add the garlic and onion to the rice when it is cooked and allow it to cool. Stir in the sultanas and pepper. Garnish with chopped spring onions. Stir in yogurt before serving.

THAI GREEN BEAN SALAD

Serves 4–6

Finely diced chicken breast or prawns, or a combination, can be added to this salad to make a hearty lunchtime or supper meal. You can find the unsweetened coconut milk, chilli paste and fish sauce at oriental food stores.

INGREDIENTS

225 g/8 oz green beans

3 tbsp grated unsweetened coconut, fresh or desiccated

100 ml/4 fl oz peanut oil

6 garlic cloves, sliced 2.5 mm/⅛-in thick lengthways

50 ml/2 fl oz fresh lime juice

50 ml/2 fl oz unsweetened coconut milk

1 tbsp roasted chilli paste (*ham prik pao*)

15 ml/1 tbsp Thai fish sauce (*nam pla*)

1 tbsp sugar

12 whole radicchio leaves

2 serrano chillies, preferably 1 red and 1 green, seeded and finely chopped

SHALLOT CROUTONS

100 ml/4 fl oz peanut oil

4 medium shallots, sliced 2.5 mm/⅛-in thick

coriander sprigs, to garnish

BLANCH THE BEANS in a saucepan of boiling, salted water for about 3 minutes, until tender but still crisp. Drain and rinse under cold running water. Cut the beans into bite-size pieces and set aside.

Heat a dry wok or small frying pant, add the grated coconut and toss gently for about 1 minute, until golden. Transfer the coconut to a plate. Pour the peanut oil into the wok and heat to 190°C/375°F using a deep-fat thermometer. Remove the wok from the heat, add the garlic slices, and stir until golden and crisp. Transfer the garlic to kitchen paper towels to drain.

In a bowl, whisk together the lime juice and coconut milk. Then whisk in one ingredient at a time: the chilli paste, fish sauce and sugar. Set aside.

Make the shallot croutons by heating the oil in a wok to 190°C/375°F (measure using a deep-fat thermometer). Remove the pan from the heat, add the shallots and stir for about 3 minutes, until the shallots are crisp and golden. Transfer to kitchen paper towels to drain. The shallot croutons can be covered and refrigerated for up to a week, but should then be lightly toasted on a baking sheet in the oven before using. Arrange the radicchio leaves on a platter or individual plates. In a large bowl, combine the beans, the toasted coconut and the garlic slices. Pour the mixture of lime juice, coconut milk, chilli paste, fish sauce and sugar over the beans, coconut and garlic. Gently fold in the serrano chillies.

THAI NOODLE SALAD IN A PEANUT DRESSING

Serves 4

The variety of textures in this dish is typical of Thai cuisine. The combination of noodles and crunchy vegetables in a nutty dressing ensures an exciting eating experience.

INGREDIENTS

450 g/1 lb thin oriental noodles

225 g/8 oz mangetout

1 red pepper, cut into strips

1 medium cucumber, thinly sliced

4 spring onions, cut diagonally into thin slices

100 g/4 oz Chinese leaves, shredded

PEANUT DRESSING

100 g/4 oz creamy peanut butter

100 ml/4 fl oz plain non-fat yogurt

15 ml/1 tbsp low-sodium soy sauce

1 garlic clove

30 ml/2 tbsp dark sesame oil

3 tbsp chopped fresh coriander

30 ml/2 tbsp rice wine vinegar

COOK THE NOODLES in a large pan of boiling water according to the packet directions, until they are tender. Drain well, transfer to a large serving bowl, and set aside. (If you are working ahead of time, toss with 15 ml/1 tbsp vegetable oil.)

Trim stalk ends of the mangetout and blanch them in boiling water for about 1 minute. Drain well and rinse in cold water; they should be bright green in colour. Add the mangetout, red peppers, cucumber and spring onions to the noodles, and toss to mix. Add the Chinese leaves and toss again gently.

In a large nonreactive bowl, stir together the peanut butter, yogurt, soy sauce, garlic, sesame oil, coriander and vinegar. Add the dressing to the salad, toss again and serve.

CORN AND KIDNEY BEAN SALAD

Serves 6

Fresh vegetables and kidney beans combine for a spicy, crunchy salad that is easy to make.

INGREDIENTS

450 g/1 lb fresh sweetcorn kernels

450-g/15-oz can kidney beans, rinsed and drained

50 g/2 oz red pepper, diced

50 g/2 oz green pepper, diced

50 g/2 oz spring onion, chopped

2 large tomatoes, seeded and chopped

15 g/½ oz fresh coriander, chopped

75 ml/3 fl oz olive oil

75 ml/3 fl oz fresh lime juice

1 clove garlic, crushed

1 tsp ground cumin

¼ tsp cayenne

½ tsp salt

¼ tsp black pepper

1 jalapeño pepper, seeded and finely chopped (optional)

COOK THE CORN, either by roasting it on the cob, or cutting it off the cob and boiling it in its own juice and a scant amount of water for about 5 minutes. Drain corn and let cool while

you mix the other ingredients.

In a large bowl, mix kidney beans, red and green peppers, spring onions, tomatoes, coriander and jalapeño if desired. Add the corn when it is cool.

In a small jar, mix the remaining ingredients. Shake well and pour over salad. The salad benefits if you prepare it several hours in advance and allow the flavours to mix.

HERBED TOMATO AND PASTA SALAD

Serves 4

Served with crusty bread, this makes a splendid starter or light lunch. It does, of course, rely on fresh basil for success.

INGREDIENTS

225 g/8 oz fresh pasta shapes

450 g/1 lb ripe tomatoes, peeled, seeded and quartered

6 spring onions, chopped

1 garlic clove, crushed

salt and freshly ground black pepper

60–90 ml/4–6 tbsp olive oil

6 basil sprigs

COOK THE PASTA in boiling salted water for 3 minutes, drain and set aside to cool. Mix the tomatoes with the spring onions. Add the garlic, seasoning and olive oil, and mix well. Cover and set aside to marinate for 1 hour.

Toss the tomato mixture into the pasta. Use scissors to shred the basil, with the soft stalk ends, over the pasta. Mix well and serve at once.

CAPELLINI AND CHILLED TOMATO SALAD

Serves 4–6

This salad combines the wonderful, sweet flavour of ripe tomatoes with the taste of chilli and other spices.

INGREDIENTS

225 g/8 oz dried capellini or spaghettini

3 large, ripe tomatoes, peeled, seeded, chopped and thoroughly drained of juices

4 garlic cloves, finely chopped

5 black olives, stoned and finely chopped

1 small hot chilli, seeded and finely chopped

15 ml/1 tbsp olive oil

juice of 1 lime

1 tbsp chopped fresh coriander

⅛ tsp salt

freshly ground black pepper

COOK THE CAPELLINI or spaghettini according to the directions on the packet and until al dente. Rinse, drain well and set aside. Mix the tomatoes and garlic together in a large bowl, then toss in the drained pasta. Refrigerate to chill thoroughly.

In a separate bowl, mix the olives, chilli, olive oil, lime juice, coriander and salt together to combine thoroughly. Add pepper to taste and set aside. Just before serving, pour the dressing over the pasta, and toss to mix well.

Herbed Tomato and Pasta Salad ▶

MEDITERRANEAN DRESSING

Makes about 250 ml/9 fl oz

Bursting with the heat-soaked flavours that result from basking in the Mediterranean sunshine, this dressing is perfect with pasta.

INGREDIENTS

2 oil-soaked sun-dried tomatoes

1 small garlic clove

1 tbsp capers

about 8 stoned black olives

22.5 ml/1½ tbsp red or white wine vinegar

105 ml/7 tbsp virgin olive oil

pinch of sugar (optional)

freshly ground black pepper

Finely chop the tomatoes, garlic, capers and olives.

Put into a bowl and add the vinegar. Slowly pour in the oil, whisking constantly, until well emulsified. Season with sugar, if using, and black pepper.

PASTA AND BEAN SALAD

Serves 4

Excellent served on the side, this salad is packed with nutritional goodness.

INGREDIENTS

225 g/8 oz spinach-flavoured fresh pasta shapes

225 g/8 oz French beans, cut into 5-cm/2-in lengths

425 g/15-oz can flageolet beans (green kidney), drained

1 red onion, halved and thinly sliced

30 ml/2 tbsp tarragon vinegar

1 tsp caster sugar

salt and freshly ground black pepper

1 garlic clove, crushed

90 ml/6 tbsp olive oil

6 tbsp croutons

Cook the pasta in boiling salted water for 3 minutes, then drain well. Place the pasta in a bowl. Blanch the French beans in boiling salted water for 3 minutes, then drain them and add them to the pasta. Stir in the flageolet beans and onion, separating the pieces as you add them to the salad.

Shake the tarragon vinegar, sugar, seasoning and garlic in a screw-top jar. When the sugar has dissolved, add the oil, put the top on the jar and shake again. Pour this dressing over the salad and toss well. Cover and leave until cold.

Just before serving, toss the salad well and mix in the croutons. Do not leave the salad to stand after the croutons are added or they will lose their crunch.

◀ *Mediterranean Dressing*

TABBOULEH

Serves 4

Although this is a simpler recipe, you may like to add seafood or other ingredients.
The salad may be made up to two days ahead and kept covered in the refrigerator.

INGREDIENTS

100 ml/4 fl oz chicken stock

100 ml/4 fl oz water

50 ml/2 fl oz fresh lemon juice

50 ml/2 fl oz olive oil

175 g/6 oz couscous, made of wheat
semolina or bulghur wheat

½ cucumber, cut
into 5-mm/¼-in pieces

2 tbsp peeled, seeded and finely
diced tomato

50 g/2 oz finely chopped spring onions

salt

1 tsp chopped fresh basil

25 g/1 oz fresh parsley, chopped

15 g/½ oz fresh mint, chopped

mint sprigs and cucumber slices,
to garnish

IN A SAUCEPAN, combine the stock, water, half the lemon juice and 15 ml/1 tbsp of the oil. Bring the mixture to the boil and stir in the couscous. Cover the pan, remove it from the heat, and leave the couscous to stand for 5 minutes. Fluff the couscous with a fork and let it cool in the pan.

In a large bowl, stir together the cucumber, tomato, spring onion, the remaining olive oil, the remaining lemon juice and salt to taste. Leave the mixture to stand for 15 minutes. Add the couscous and herbs, stirring well to mix. Cover the salad and refrigerate for 1 hour before serving. Garnish with mint sprigs and cucumber slices.

VEGETABLE SALADS

ITALIAN SALAD ON CROSTINI

Serves 4

This flavourful salad, spread on toasted bread, makes a nice change from green salads served on a plate or in a bowl.
The salad-topped crostini can also be served as an appetizer.

INGREDIENTS

1 large wholemeal baguette,
cut on the diagonal into 12 slices

2 garlic cloves, peeled and cut in half

15 ml/1 tbsp olive oil or vegetable oil

1 yellow pepper, cored, seeded
and cut into 2.5-cm/1-in cubes

2 green peppers, cored, seeded
and cut into short strips
about 2.5 cm/1-in long

1 long fresh red chilli,
seeded and finely chopped

½ medium onion, thinly sliced

2 medium tomatoes,
seeded and cut into 2.5-cm/1-in cubes

1 cup fresh basil leaves, chopped

1 tbsp chopped fresh oregano

30 ml/2 tbsp balsamic or red wine vinegar

¾ tsp salt

½ tsp freshly ground black pepper

fresh basil leaves, to garnish

PREHEAT THE GRILL. Arrange the bread slices on a grill pan. Rub garlic cloves on the bread. Discard the garlic. Grill the bread, 7.5 cm/3 in from the heat, for 4 minutes or until browned, turning them over halfway through and watching closely.

Heat the oil in a nonstick medium frying pan over medium heat. Add the yellow and green peppers, chilli and onion. Cook, covered, for almost 15 minutes, stirring occasionally. Remove from heat. Stir in the tomatoes, basil leaves, fresh oregano, vinegar and salt and pepper until combined. Spoon salad evenly over the crostini and garnish with the fresh basil leaves. Serve immediately.

CHICORY, WALNUT AND ORANGE SALAD

Serves 4–6

A classic salad recipe, the fine blend of chicory, walnut and sweet oranges makes an ideal appetizer or side salad.

INGREDIENTS

4 plump heads chicory

2 large sweet oranges

75 g/3 oz walnut halves

45 ml/3 tbsp olive or walnut oil

15 ml/1 tbsp lemon juice

1 garlic clove, finely crushed

½ tsp sugar

Wash the chicory heads thoroughly and pat dry with kitchen paper towels. Cut into 1-cm/½-in slices.

Peel and slice the oranges – or divide them into segments – removing the skin and pith from each. Coarsely chop the walnuts, reserving a few for decoration. Place the chicory, orange and walnuts in a bowl and mix.

Mix the olive or walnut oil, lemon juice, garlic and sugar, and pour this dressing over the combined chicory, orange and walnuts.

Decorate with the reserved walnuts. Serve chilled.

WATERCRESS SALAD WITH ZINGY PEPPER DRESSING

Serves 4

This is not for those who like tame, bland salads. This one has the bite of watercress, the sweetness of
fresh tomato and a delectable mustardy hot pepper heat. It will enliven any plain main dish.

INGREDIENTS

2 bunches watercress, washed,
trimmed and dried

1 large ripe tomato, cut into
bite-size pieces

1 small onion, thinly sliced, rings
separated

15 ml/1 tbsp red wine vinegar

15 ml/1 tbsp chicken stock

15 ml/1 tbsp hot pepper sauce

½ tsp crushed garlic

¼ tsp French mustard

salt and freshly ground black pepper

IN A LARGE bowl, combine the
watercress, tomato and onion. In a
small bowl, whisk together the vinegar,
chicken stock, hot pepper sauce, garlic
and mustard. Season with salt and
pepper. Drizzle over the salad and toss
gently to coat.

ZESTY ASPARAGUS SALAD

Serves 4

The slight sharpness of the mustard in this salad accents the delicate flavour of the asparagus, without overwhelming it.
It is an adaptation of several French recipes. Use only the hard-boiled egg white if you are concerned about cholesterol.
The vinaigrette may be made up to two days in advance.

INGREDIENTS

450 g/1 lb asparagus

4–8 large lettuce leaves

1 hard-boiled egg, finely chopped

ZESTY VINAIGRETTE

175 ml/6 fl oz rapeseed or mild olive oil

30 ml/2 tbsp red wine vinegar

1 tsp dry mustard
or 2 tsp Dijon mustard

¼ tsp black pepper

⅛ tsp salt

1 large garlic clove, crushed

2 tbsp snipped fresh chives

TRIM THE ENDS of the asparagus.
Soak the stalks in cold water to
remove any dirt, then drain. Bring a
large flat pan of water to the boil, add
the asparagus, and cook for
5–7 minutes until tender-crisp.
Alternatively, steam in a large covered
pan with about 1 cm/½ in boiling salted
water for 12–15 minutes. Remove
each stalk with tongs. Drain and rinse
immediately under cold running water.

Drain again, wrap in kitchen paper towels, and chill in the refrigerator for about 2 hours.

Prepare the vinaigrette. Place the oil, vinegar, mustard, pepper, salt, garlic and chives in a jar with a tightly fitting lid, and shake until thoroughly blended. Refrigerate for 2 hours before using.

To serve, line 1–2 lettuce leaves on each of four plates. Divide the chilled asparagus between the plates, and spoon over 15 ml/1 tbsp of vinaigrette on each plate. Sprinkle the salads with the hard-boiled egg, and serve.

GREEK SALAD

Serves 4

This simple but popular salad combines crisp cucumber and cherry tomatoes with soft, crumbly feta cheese.

INGREDIENTS

10 ml/2 tsp red wine vinegar

½ tsp sugar

30 ml/2 tbsp olive oil

salt and freshly ground black pepper

1 cucumber

350 g/12 oz cherry tomatoes, quartered

100 g/4 oz feta cheese, crumbled

15–25 g/½–1 oz fresh basil, finely chopped

IN A LARGE bowl, whisk together the vinegar, sugar, olive oil and salt and pepper to taste. Peel the cucumber, halve it lengthways, and remove the seeds. Cut crossways into 5-mm/¼-in slices. Add to the bowl with the tomatoes, feta cheese and basil. Toss the salad well to combine, and serve.

SAKE-SOAKED MUSHROOMS

Serves 4

This Japanese-style salad makes a light, refreshing accompaniment to grilled meat, fish and shellfish dishes.
The salad will keep well for two days in the refrigerator.

INGREDIENTS

225 ml/8 fl oz sake

22.5 ml/1½ tbsp soy sauce

15 ml/1 tbsp rice wine vinegar

1 tbsp sugar

5 large thin slices fresh ginger root

1 large garlic clove, finely chopped

450 g/1 lb large mushrooms, rinsed, stalks removed and thinly sliced

5 ml/1 tsp dark sesame oil

COMBINE THE SAKE, soy sauce, rice wine vinegar, sugar, ginger and garlic in a medium nonreactive saucepan. Bring to the boil over a medium heat. Add the mushrooms and reduce the heat to medium-low, simmer for 25 minutes, until the liquid is almost evaporated. Remove from the heat and discard the ginger. Stir in the sesame oil. Set aside to cool to room temperature. Cover, refrigerate and serve cold.

◄ *Greek Salad*

RUSSIAN DILLED POTATO SALAD

Serves 4

A Russian immigrant to my home state of Ohio introduced this elegant yet hearty peasant dish to the region. Substituting non-fat or low-fat soured cream and yogurt will reduce calories and cholesterol with little loss in flavour. The chervil will add a subtle anise flavor, but omit the herb if you do not like its unique taste.

INGREDIENTS

30 ml/2 tbsp white wine vinegar

30 ml/2 tbsp cider vinegar

1 tbsp brown sugar

1 tsp salt

1 tsp dry chervil (optional)

1 tsp coarse-grain mustard

225 g/8 oz cucumber, peeled, seeded and diced

225 ml/8 fl oz plain yogurt

225 ml/8 fl oz soured cream

15 ml/1 tbsp fresh lemon or lime juice

1 tbsp dried dill

8 medium new, red potatoes

salt

mild sweet paprika

IN A LARGE nonreactive bowl, mix together the vinegars, brown sugar, salt, chervil, mustard, cucumber, yogurt, soured cream, lemon juice and dill. Cover and refrigerate.

Wash the potatoes well, gently scrubbing so the skin remains intact. Place potatoes in a large saucepan, cover with water, and bring to the boil. Cook over a medium-high heat for 10–15 minutes, or until tender. Cool under cold running water and drain well. Cut each potato into bite-size pieces. Fold the potatoes into the chilled yogurt and soured cream mixture with a wooden or plastic spoon. Refrigerate for at least 6 hours to let the flavours blend. Season with salt and paprika to taste before serving.

SPINACH AND FIG SALAD

Serves 4

A refreshing salad that takes just minutes to prepare.

INGREDIENTS

450 g/1 lb fresh spinach, washed

25 g/1 oz pine kernels

3 fresh figs

60 ml/4 tbsp lemon dressing

a few fresh nasturtium flowers
(optional)

REMOVE AND DISCARD any coarse stems from the spinach and tear the leaves into pieces. Place in a colander to drain well. Place the pine kernels in a small, dry pan and roast until lightly browned, stirring. Remove from the pan and leave to cool.

Wash the figs, trim off the stalks, cut each into quarters and then into thin slices. Place the spinach, pine kernels and figs into a serving bowl. Sprinkle over the dressing, toss well and garnish with a few fresh nasturtium flowers, if available.

ARMENIAN AUBERGINE SALAD

Serves 4–6

Aubergine recipes are surprisingly similar the world over. Hungarians like just a hint of sweetness in theirs, so add a pinch of sugar if you find this recipe too tart. The garnishes will add some needed colour to the dish.

INGREDIENTS

2 aubergines

olive oil for brushing

1 medium onion, chopped

15 g/½ oz fresh parsley, finely chopped

2 tsp salt

1 tsp black pepper

100 ml/4 fl oz olive oil

150 ml/¼ pint vinegar

lettuce leaves

tomato wedges or cherry tomatoes and stoned black olives, to garnish

PREHEAT THE GRILL to hot. Remove the stalk from the aubergine and slice the aubergine into thick rounds. Brush a little olive oil on the aubergine slices, place on a wire rack and grill for 3–5 minutes on each side, until soft. Leave to cool, then peel and chop. Mix the aubergine with the onion and parsley in a large bowl. Add the salt and pepper. Whisk the oil and vinegar together in a small bowl, and add to the aubergine mixture. Toss well to coat evenly. Serve the salad on a bed of lettuce leaves, and garnish with tomato wedges or cherry tomatoes and olives.

◀ *Spinach and Fig Salad*

ORIGINAL CAESAR

Serves 4

Here's a salad that really is fit for movie stars. In the 1920s, Hollywood actors used to dash across the border to
Tijuana, Mexico to dine at restaurants owned by an Italian immigrant named Caesar Cardini.
He whipped up this extravaganza for them and they began demanding it in restaurants back home.
Today, it is served in fine dining establishments the world over.

INGREDIENTS

1 egg (see page 18)

¼ tsp salt

¼ tsp freshly ground black pepper

30 ml/2 tbsp white wine vinegar

1 clove garlic, peeled and crushed

½ tsp Dijon mustard

5 ml/1 tsp Worcestershire sauce

2 anchovies, finely chopped

30 ml/2 tbsp fresh lemon juice

100 ml/4 fl oz extra virgin olive oil

1 Cos lettuce, rinsed, dried,
torn into bite-size pieces and chilled

50 g/2 oz Parmesan cheese,
freshly grated

4 anchovy strips, to garnish

PARMESAN CROUTONS

22.5 ml/1½ tbsp olive oil

1 large clove garlic

50 g/2 oz French or Italian-style bread,
cubed

15 g/½ oz Parmesan cheese,
freshly grated

COOK THE EGG in its shell in simmering water for about 1½ minutes and set aside until cool enough to handle. In a large bowl combine the salt, pepper, vinegar, garlic, mustard, Worcestershire sauce and chopped anchovies.

Break the egg into a small bowl and sprinkle the lemon juice over it. Whisk until frothy and pour mixture into the larger bowl containing the salt, pepper, vinegar, garlic, mustard, Worcestershire sauce and chopped anchovies. Continue whisking while gradually adding in the olive oil.

Make the Parmesan Croutons by heating the oil and garlic in a heavy frying pan until the garlic has turned golden. Discard the garlic. Add the bread cubes and cook, stirring for 3–5 minutes until lightly browned; toss cubes in Parmesan cheese.

Add lettuce, grated Parmesan cheese and croutons to the large bowl. Toss gently to coat the salad greens. Place anchovy strips artfully across top of serving bowl or divide salad on to four platters and place an anchovy strip across the top of each. Serve immediately.

Note: Pregnant women and persons with concerns about eggs should substitute pasteurized egg product for the raw egg.

ROAST TOMATO AND GARLIC VINAIGRETTE

Makes about 225 ml/6 fl oz

Pour the dressing over grilled red peppers, courgettes, aubergines and onions or toss with pasta.

INGREDIENTS

1 large ridged tomato

3 plump garlic cloves, unpeeled

5 ml/1 tsp sherry vinegar

60 ml/4 tbsp virgin olive oil

salt and freshly ground black pepper

Preheat the grill. Grill the tomato and garlic until softened, charred and blistered. Leave to cool then peel them. Seed and chop the tomato.

Put the garlic and tomato into a blender and mix until smooth. Add the vinegar then, with the motor running, slowly pour in the oil until well emulsified. Season.

LOW-CAL COLESLAW

Serves 4

The name 'cole' in coleslaw comes from a Dutch word meaning 'cabbage'. For a heartier version of this light salad, add some cauliflower florets and diced courgettes.

INGREDIENTS

60–70 ml/4–5 tbsp mayonnaise

50 ml/2 fl oz plain non-fat or low-fat yogurt

30 ml/2 tbsp cider, rice wine or tarragon vinegar

2 tsp dry mustard

1 tsp sugar

½ tsp salt

1.25 ml/¼ tsp Tabasco or other hot pepper sauce

575 g/1¼ lb green cabbage, shredded

100 g/4 oz red or green pepper, chopped

2 carrots, peeled and grated

75 g/3 oz spring onions, sliced

Mix THE MAYONNAISE, yogurt, vinegar, mustard, sugar, salt and Tabasco in a medium bowl to combine. Add the cabbage, pepper, carrots and spring onions and toss well to coat evenly. Cover and refrigerate for up to 3 days, stirring thoroughly before serving.

◀ *Roast Tomato and Garlic Vinaigrette*

FRESH & FRUITY SALADS

TAMARILLO AND AVOCADO COCKTAIL

Serves 4

Tamarillos can now be found in most supermarkets or grocery shops. They give this simple salad an exotic taste.

INGREDIENTS

2 large ripe avocados

3 tamarillos

shredded lettuce

150 g/5 oz packet soft cheese with herbs and garlic

90 ml/6 tbsp Greek yogurt or soured cream

1 tsp caster sugar

3 spring onions, chopped

QUARTER AND PEEL the avocados and slice them across. Peel the tamarillos thinly, halve them lengthways and slice across. Arrange a little shredded lettuce on four individual plates.

Mix the cheese with the yogurt or soured cream in a bowl. Sprinkle the caster sugar over the tamarillos, mix in the chopped spring onion and leave to stand for 15 minutes.

Arrange the avocado slices on the lettuce, top with the tamarillo mixture and spoon the cheese and yogurt dressing over the top.

DRUNKEN BANANA SALAD

Serves 4

Here is a sweet, lazy-day treat. With its luscious fruit and coconut, this salad will remind you of a tropical island.

INGREDIENTS

2 bananas

2 oranges

40 g/1 ½ oz desiccated coconut

50 ml/2 fl oz brandy

50 ml/2 fl oz dark rum

1 tsp sugar

PEEL THE BANANAS and cut them into rounds. Peel the oranges and divide into segments. Alternate slices of bananas, orange segments and dried coconut in a fruit dish until full. Mix the brandy and rum with the sugar, pour over the salad, and serve.

Tamarillo and Avocado Cocktail ▶

FRESH FRUIT WITH PEACH GLAZE

Serves 4

This salad will bring summer indoors, even in the middle of winter.

INGREDIENTS

225 ml/8 fl oz fruit juice, such as peach, pineapple-orange-guava, pineapple-orange-banana, mandarin orange, or raspberry

7.5 ml/½ tbsp lemon juice

1½ tbsp sugar

¼ tsp finely grated lemon rind

½ tbsp cornflour

100 g/4 oz fresh pineapple, cubed

100 g/4 oz bananas, sliced

75 g/3 oz cantaloupe melon, cubed

75 g/3 oz kiwi fruit, cubed

75 g/3 oz nectarines, sliced

mint leaves, to decorate

COMBINE THE FRUIT juice, lemon juice, sugar, lemon rind and cornflour in a medium saucepan. Stir over a medium-high heat for 5 minutes, or until the mixture comes to the boil. Reduce the heat to low and cook for 2 minutes more, or until slightly thickened. Remove from the heat and leave to cool slightly; alternatively, refrigerate the glaze until thoroughly chilled.

To serve, arrange the fruit in four dessert dishes. Spoon the glaze over the fruit, and decorate with mint leaves.

HAWAIIAN MACADAMIA SALAD

Serves 4–6

This zesty salad is accented by peppery paw-paw seeds and sweet, rich macadamia nuts.
It can be combined with grilled, shelled prawns to make a delectable entrée.

INGREDIENTS

1 ripe paw-paw, quartered lengthways with seeds reserved

1 ripe avocado, peeled, stoned and cut into bite-size pieces

175–225 g/6–8 oz bite-size pieces of lettuce

25 g/1 oz toasted macadamia nuts

DRESSING

2 tbsp paw-paw seeds, measured out from the reserved seeds

50 ml/2 fl oz rapeseed oil

15 ml/1 tbsp lemon juice

1½ tsp Dijon mustard

1 tsp grated, peeled fresh ginger

salt and freshly ground pepper

PLACE THE PAW-PAW in a covered nonreactive bowl, or in a heavy-duty resealable plastic bag, and refrigerate to chill.

Prepare the dressing. Place the paw-paw seeds in a processor or blender.

Add the oil, lemon juice, mustard, ginger, salt and pepper. Process until the seeds are the size of coarsely crushed black pepper. Set aside.

Peel the avocado, remove the stone, and cut into bite-size pieces. Transfer to a large bowl and add the lettuce. Pour over the dressing and toss to mix and coat evenly. Arrange on serving plates, top with the paw-paw, and sprinkle with the toasted macadamia nuts. Serve immediately.

TROPICAL FRUIT SALAD

Serves 6

This deliciously sweet dessert is supremely satisfying.

INGREDIENTS

1 fresh pineapple, peeled and sliced, or 1 x 400-g/14-oz tin pineapple slices

45 ml/3 tbsp rum

40 g/1½ oz brown sugar

juice of 1 lemon

2 bananas, sliced

2 mangoes, sliced

2 ripe guavas, sliced

5 tbsp grated fresh coconut meat

½ tsp freshly grated nutmeg

PUT THE PINEAPPLE slices into a glass bowl. Add the rum and sugar and chill, covered, for 1 hour.

Pour in the lemon juice and mix in all the fruit. Serve sprinkled with the grated coconut and nutmeg.

STAR FRUIT AND ROCKET SALAD WITH RASPBERRY VINEGAR DRESSING

Serves 4

This makes a very good side salad or appetizer. Rocket has a strong, very distinctive flavor which is excellent when balanced with sweet salad greens such as iceberg or romaine lettuce, but do not be tempted to add too much rocket or cut it too coarsely as it will overpower the other delicate ingredients, especially the star fruit.

If rocket is not available a bunch or two of watercress may be used instead.

INGREDIENTS

½ iceberg lettuce, shredded

12 medium rocket leaves, finely shredded

3 scallions or green onions, chopped

2 star fruit, sliced and quartered

DRESSING

3 tbsp raspberry vinegar

1 tsp superfine sugar

salt and freshly ground black pepper

8 tbsp olive oil

TOSS THE LETTUCE, rocket, and scallions together in a salad bowl. Next make the dressing: place the vinegar in a basin and whisk in the superfine sugar with plenty of seasoning. Continue the whisking until the sugar and salt have dissolved. Slowly add the olive oil, whisking all the time to combine the ingredients well.

Add the star fruit to the salad. Pour the dressing over and mix lightly. Serve at once. Do not leave the star fruit to stand for any length of time once it is cut as it dries on the surface and tends to discolor slightly around the edges.

MINTY MELON MEDLEY

Serves 4

This adaptation of a Pennsylvania-Dutch recipe makes excellent use of delicious summer fruits.

INGREDIENTS

1 honeydew melon, cut into bite-size chunks

1 cantaloupe, cut into bite-size chunks

1 pint blackberries, blueberries, raspberries, or other in-season berries

10-oz jar mint jelly

½ cup chopped fresh mint

¼ cup sugar

¼ cup water

mint sprigs, to decorate

Equally divide the melon chunks and berries between four bowls, and stir gently to mix. Cover and chill for at least 2 hours. Meanwhile, melt the mint jelly in the top of a double boiler. Stir in the chopped mint, sugar, and water. Transfer the mint mixture to a small bowl, cover, and refrigerate for about 1 hour, until well chilled. To serve, decorate the fruit salads with mint sprigs, and serve with the mint syrup.

Star Fruit and Rocket Salad with Raspberry Vinegar Dressing ▶

PAW-PAW-CITRUS SALAD WITH PAW-PAW SEED DRESSING

Serves 4

This cool and refreshing salad is a nice foil for a spicy jerked dish.

INGREDIENTS

1 small red onion,
halved and thinly sliced

1 orange, separated into segments,
with 30 ml/2 tbsp juice reserved

2 grapefruits, preferably pink,
separated into segments

½ ripe paw-paw (about 225 g/8 oz),
coarsely sliced

1 red pepper, cored,
seeded and thinly sliced

1 yellow pepper, cored,
seeded and thinly sliced

DRESSING

60 g/ 2½ oz granulated sugar

1½ tsp salt

¼ tsp French mustard

45 ml/3 tbsp white vinegar

100 ml/4 fl oz vegetable oil

2 tbsp paw-paw seeds

PLACE THE ONION in a small bowl. Cover with ice water and leave to stand for 30 minutes at room temperature. Drain and dry on absorbent kitchen paper towels.

Combine the orange and grapefruit segments with the onion, paw-paw, red pepper, and yellow pepper in a large salad bowl.

In a blender or food processor, blend together the sugar, salt, mustard and vinegar until blended well. With the motor running, add the oil in a stream and blend until smooth. Add the seeds and blend until they are about the size of peppercorns. Drizzle the dressing over the salad and toss well.

JAPANESE GREEN FRUIT SALAD

Serves 6–8

This is a refreshing salad made with exotic fruits of the same colour mixed with fragrant jelly cubes of elderflower.

INGREDIENTS
FOR THE JELLY

6 leaves of gelatine

450 ml/¾ pint water

150 ml/¼ pint elderflower cordial

FOR THE SUGAR SYRUP

175 g/6 oz granulated sugar

450 ml/¾ pint water

FOR THE FRUIT

1 small melon

3 kiwi fruit

175 g/6 oz green grapes

1 green apple

2 guavas

SOAK THE GELATINE in half the water for 15 minutes. Add the remaining water, place in a saucepan and heat gently to dissolve. Allow to cool slightly before adding the cordial. Rinse an 18-cm/7-in shallow square tin with water and pour in the jelly mixture. Leave in a cold place to set.

To make the syrup, put the sugar and water in a saucepan and heat until the sugar has dissolved. Boil rapidly for 2–3 minutes until slightly syrupy. Remove from the heat and let cool.

Cut the melon into balls or cubes and place in a large serving bowl. Peel and slice the kiwi fruit. Wash the grapes, halve, and seed if necessary. Wash and core the apple and cut into slices. Add all these fruits to the bowl with the cooled syrup. Peel the guavas, halve and scoop out the seeds. Slice and add to the salad.

Quickly dip the tin of jelly into hot water and turn out on to damp greaseproof paper. Cut into cubes. Add to salad just before serving.

ISLAND FRUIT SALAD

Serves 4

Add prawns to the marinade and this becomes a regal salad.

INGREDIENTS

15 ml/1 tbsp balsamic vinegar

juice from 1 orange

10 ml/2 tsp soy sauce

30 ml/2 tbsp vegetable oil

¼ tsp salt

½ tsp granulated sugar (optional)

2 medium oranges,
peeled and separated into segments,
reserving juice

1 x 150-g/5-oz can unsweetened
grapefruit segments, drained

1 starfruit, kiwi fruit or
pear, sliced

1 lb cooked prawns,
shelled and deveined

1 medium red onion, thinly sliced

lettuce leaves or two avocados,
to garnish (optional)

IN A BLENDER or food processor or by hand, blend the balsamic vinegar, orange juice, soy sauce, oil, salt and sugar until smooth. Transfer to a bowl and add the orange and grapefruit segments, starfruit, kiwi or pear slices, prawns and onion. Marinate, covered, in the refrigerator for 1 hour. Drain the fruit and onion of liquid and serve on lettuce-lined plates or in halved, stoned avocados, partially scooped out.

PASSION FRUIT CUP

Serves 4

This recipe is from J. R. Brooks & Son of Homestead, Florida, one of the foremost growers of tropical fruits and vegetables in the United States.

INGREDIENTS

4 passion fruit, tops cut and pulp scooped out

1 banana, sliced

1 large kiwi fruit, peeled, halved and cut into semicircles

30 ml/2 tbsp honey

100 g/4 oz seedless red grapes, halved

squirt of juice from 1 Key or regular lime

COMBINE FRUITS WITH honey. Add 1–2 squeezes lime juice to taste, and serve.

MANGO-STARFRUIT SALAD WITH GINGER VINAIGRETTE

Serves 4

This vinaigrette tastes great sprinkled over boniato chips, fried green plantains, green salads, and even jerk dishes.

INGREDIENTS

4 mangoes, cubed

4 starfruits, sliced crossways for star shapes

15 g/½ oz ginger root, grated

100 ml/4 fl oz olive oil

100 ml/4 fl oz cider vinegar

30 ml/2 tbsp fresh lime juice

1 tsp French mustard

1 tsp minced fresh coriander

¼ tsp minced spring onion

¼ tsp salt

¼ tsp freshly ground black pepper

COMBINE THE MANGOES and starfruit and chill. Purée the ginger, olive oil, vinegar, lime juice, mustard, coriander, spring onion, salt and pepper until smooth in a food processor or blender or by hand. Drizzle over the chilled fruit.

JAPANESE PERSIMMON SALAD

Serves 4

This gorgeous deep-orange fruit is cultivated primarily in Japan and China but persimmons are also grown in California, France, Spain, Italy, North Africa and Chile.

INGREDIENTS

4 tbsp whole unblanched almonds

4 ripe persimmons

40 ml/8 tsp hazelnut or almond liqueur

bunch of small grapes
or sliced fresh fig, to garnish

PREHEAT THE OVEN to 170°C/325°F/ Gas Mark 3. Place the almonds in a baking dish and bake for 15 minutes, until lightly golden inside. Cool, then chop in coarse slivers.

Gently cut out the leaf-stemmed end from each persimmon and discard. Halve each fruit lengthways and place on a serving dish. With a sharp paring knife, deeply score a diamond pattern into the flesh, reaching almost to the skin. Drizzle the liqueur slowly over each persimmon half, squeezing the fruit gently to open the interstices. Sprinkle with the chopped almonds. Place several grapes or fig slices In the leaf cavity of each persimmon half, and serve.

FROMAGE FRAIS WITH PASSION FRUIT

Serves 3–4

A refreshing snack that is quick to prepare and nutritious.

INGREDIENTS

225 g/8 oz fromage frais

2–3 passion fruit

50 g/2 oz cashew nuts

sugar to taste (optional)

lettuce and cucumber, to garnish

PLACE THE FROMAGE frais in a bowl. Halve the passion fruit and stir in with the nuts. Add sugar, if liked. Spoon into 4 lettuce leaves garnished with cucumber and serve with warm brown rolls.

Japanese Persimmon Salad ▶

STUFFED FIGS WITH PLUMS

Serves 4

This can be made with apricots, small pears or other suitable fruits that are not too large.

INGREDIENTS

50 g/2 oz chopped almonds

125 g/4 oz lean bacon

125 g/4 oz cream cheese

1 tbsp chopped chives

freshly ground pepper

4 figs

8 plums

lollo rosso lettuce, to garnish

PLACE THE ALMONDS either in a dry frying pan or in a grill pan, with the rack removed, and toast to brown lightly. Remove and cool.

Fry or grill the bacon until crisp, drain on kitchen paper towels and chop into pieces. Soften the cheese in a bowl and add the almonds, bacon, chives and pepper.

Cut the stalks off the figs and cut down into each fig twice, not cutting completely through. Open out so that there are four wedges. Place a fig on each of four plates and put a little of the cheese mixture in the centre of each fruit. Cut the plums in half, remove the stones and divide the remaining cheese mixture between them. Arrange four halves round each fig and garnish with a little lollo rosso lettuce.

ORANGE SALAD

Serves 6–8

Oranges in North Africa, especially Morocco, are wonderfully sweet and juicy. They are used to make many different refreshing salads for serving at the beginning and end of a meal.

INGREDIENTS

6 ripe oranges, peeled and thinly sliced horizontally

12 fresh dates, stoned and thinly sliced

12 blanched almonds, slivered

15–30 ml/1–2 tbsp orange-flower water

ground cinnamon for sprinkling

PLACE THE ORANGE slices on a shallow serving plate. Scatter over the dates and almonds and sprinkle over orange-flower water. Finally, sprinkle with ground cinnamon. Cover and chill lightly.

◀ *Stuffed Figs with Plums*

EASY AMBROSIA SALAD

Serves 4

This extravagant version of ambrosia includes kiwi fruit and strawberries in addition to the classic ingredients of oranges and coconut.

INGREDIENTS

30 ml/2 tbsp plain low-fat yogurt or buttermilk

15 ml/1 tbsp maple syrup

175–225 g/6–8 oz strawberries, hulled and quartered

1 navel orange, peeled and chopped

2 kiwi fruit, peeled and chopped

25 g/1 oz sweetened, flaked coconut

GENTLY MIX THE yogurt or buttermilk, maple syrup, strawberries, orange, kiwi fruit and coconut together in a bowl, and serve.

ORANGE SALAD WITH GARLIC AND RED WINE

Serves 4

A hot weather salad, which also shows the strong connections of the west of Spain with the south. It is really a salad of left-overs, but can be very colourful.

INGREDIENTS

6 oranges

1 big juicy lemon

2 hard-boiled eggs, peeled

3 ends of *chorizo* sausage (or 1–2 thick salami slices)

1–2 garlic cloves, finely chopped

salt

100–125 ml/3½–4fl oz red wine

60–75 ml/4–5 tbsp olive oil

handful of green olives

PEEL AND SLICE the oranges and lemon: 15 minutes chilling in freezer first helps to cut perfect round slices. Then discard the pips, and put in a shallow dish.

Chop the egg white and *chorizo* or salami. Mash the garlic in a mortar (or on a board with the flat of the knife) and add a pinch of salt. Work in the hard egg yolk (in the mortar or a cup) and then the wine and oil. Pour over the salad. Scatter with egg white, sausage, and olives.

Easy Ambrosia Salad ▶

CRANBERRY SALAD

Serves 4

I always think of Thanksgiving when it comes to cranberries, but this fruit salad can be served any time of the year. The salad would look especially pretty at Christmas in a wreath-shaped mould and garnished with fresh mint leaves.

INGREDIENTS

100 g/4 oz fresh cranberries, finely ground in food processor

about 75 g/3 oz miniature marshmallows

50 g/2 oz granulated sugar

100 g/4 oz tart apples, such as Granny Smith or pippin apples, diced, unpeeled

25 g/1 oz seedless grapes, halved

25 g/1 oz pecans, chopped

100ml/4 fl oz double cream, whipped

PLACE THE CRANBERRIES in a food processor or blender and process. In a large mixing bowl, combine the cranberries, marshmallows and sugar. Refrigerate overnight. The next day, add the apples, grapes and pecans to the bowl and mix well. Fold in the whipped cream and serve immediately.

PAW-PAW AND STRAWBERRY SALAD

Serves 4

Low in calories, this sweet-tasting salad makes a perfect side salad or light meal.

INGREDIENTS

1 medium-sized ripe paw-paw

125 g/4 oz fresh strawberries, hulled

7-cm/3-in piece cucumber

90 ml/6 tbsp orange-flavored vinaigrette dressing

watercress, to garnish

CUT THE PAW-PAW into quarters, remove the skin and seeds, and slice the flesh into a serving dish. Cut the strawberries into quarters or halves, if large, and add to the paw-paw. Peel the cucumber and cut into slices. Add to the fruits with the dressing. Toss gently and serve slightly chilled, garnished with watercress.

◄ *Cranberry Salad*

AVOCADO AND APPLE SALAD

Serves 4

Composed of just four ingredients, this simple salad is ideal for serving with a rich main course.

INGREDIENTS

2 ripe avocados

2 small eating apples

60 ml/4 tbsp vinaigrette dressing

1 tbsp freshly chopped parsley

PEEL OFF THE green skins of the avocados, cut in half and remove the stones. Slice the flesh thinly and place in a bowl. Wash the apples, quarter and core, dice and add to the avocado with the dressing and chopped parsley.

COSTA DEL SOL COOLER

Serves 4

Here's a refreshing, moulded, gazpacho-style dish influenced by the famous cold soup of Costa del Sol in Spain. Use a light or non-fat prepared mayonnaise if you wish to cut down on calories and dairy fat.

INGREDIENTS

350 ml/12 fl oz tomato juice

1 x 7-g/¼-oz envelope unflavored gelatine

15 ml/1 tbsp cider vinegar

15 ml/1 tbsp lemon juice

⅛ tsp garlic powder

¾ tsp salt

⅛ tsp black pepper

⅛ tsp Tabasco or other hot pepper sauce

350 g/12 oz tomatoes, peeled and diced

50 g/2 oz cucumber, finely chopped

25 g/1 oz green pepper, finely chopped

15 g/½ oz onion, finely chopped

15 g/½ oz celery, finely chopped

75 ml/5 tbsp soured cream

75 ml/5 tbsp prepared or homemade mayonnaise

POUR THE TOMATO juice into a saucepan, and stir in the gelatine. Leave to stand for 2 minutes. Bring to a simmer over a medium-low heat, and stir until the gelatine has dissolved. Add the vinegar, lemon juice, garlic powder, salt, black pepper and Tabasco, and mix well. Transfer to a large bowl and refrigerate until the mixture has thickened slightly.

Then add the tomatoes, cucumber, green pepper, onion and celery to the tomato juice mixture. Pour into a lightly oiled 1.4 L/2½ pint ring mould and chill until firm. Meanwhile, combine the soured cream and mayonnaise, and chill.

To serve, unmould the salad on to a large serving plate and mound a spoonful of the soured cream mixture in the centre.

ORANGE AND WATERCRESS SALAD IN CITRUS DRESSING

Serves 4

This refreshing fruit salad has a Caribbean flair, but the ingredients are easily available.

INGREDIENTS

1 large bunch watercress

2 medium oranges, peeled, seeded, segmented and sliced crossways

40 g/1½ oz spring onions, sliced

CITRUS DRESSING

22.5 ml/1½ tbsp fresh lemon juice

15 ml/1 tbsp orange juice

¼ tsp crushed dried mint

30 ml/2 tbsp olive oil

¼ tsp salt

RINSE THE WATERCRESS well. Remove and discard large stalks, dry the leaves on kitchen paper towels, and refrigerate until chilled. To serve, place the watercress in a bowl or on a plate. Add orange segments and spring onions. In a small bowl, mix all ingredients together to combine. Pour the dressing over the salad and toss gently. Serve immediately.

FAMOUS WALDORF SALAD

Serves 4

A simpler version of this salad was created by chef Oscar Tschirky in the 1890s for a party to celebrate the impending opening of the Waldorf-Astoria Hotel in New York. The recipe is included in this chapter because the salad really became popular when walnuts were added some years later. The tropical fruit and coconut are new additions, and give the salad a Caribbean touch.

INGREDIENTS

150 g/5 oz tart apples, diced

150 g/5 oz seedless green grapes, or 2 × 225-g/8-oz cans tropical fruit salad, drained

2 tbsp desiccated coconut (optional)

75 g/3 oz stoned dates, chopped (optional)

40 g/1½ oz celery, diced

150 ml/¼ pint mayonnaise, plain yogurt or buttermilk

15 ml/1 tbsp walnut oil

10 ml/2 tsp fresh lemon or lime juice

1 tsp sugar

¼ tsp ground ginger

50 g/2 oz walnuts, chopped

IN A LARGE bowl, mix together the apples, grapes or tropical fruit, desiccated coconut, dates and celery. In a separate bowl, whisk together the mayonnaise, walnut oil, lemon or lime juice, sugar and ginger. Pour the mixture over the salad and lightly toss. Cover and refrigerate. Just before serving, gently mix in the walnuts.

PEACH SALAD

Serves 4

The ancient Persians brought peaches to North Africa, as well as melons and pomegranates. I like to eat this light, delicately-perfumed fruit salad on its own, but it can be served with crème fraîche, cream, thick yogurt or ice cream.

INGREDIENTS

4 large ripe peaches, peeled if liked, and sliced

about 3 tbsp sugar

10–20 ml/2–4 tsp rose or orange-flower water

mint leaves, to decorate, if liked

PUT THE PEACH slices in a shallow serving dish, sprinkle over the sugar and rose or orange-flower water and mix together gently. Cover and chill for 2 hours. Just before serving, scatter over a few mint leaves, if liked.

Famous Waldorf Salad ▶

CREAMY ORANGE AND CHICORY SALAD

Serves 4

Inspired by a German recipe, this salad combines the sweetness of cream and oranges
with the bite of chicory, mustard and pepper.

INGREDIENTS

2 large heads chicory

1 seedless orange

115 ml/4 fl oz cream

1 tbsp mustard

salt and pepper

REMOVE THE OUTER leaves of the chicory, using only the white leaves. Cut the leaves in half lengthways and arrange on a serving platter. Peel the orange, removing the white pith. Finely grate the rind and blanch for 5 minutes to eliminate any bitterness. Drain, pat dry with a kitchen paper towel, and set aside to cool.

Mix the cream with the mustard, and season with salt and pepper to taste. Pour over the chicory. Sprinkle the grated orange rind on top. Slice the remaining orange flesh and use to garnish the salad.

STRAWBERRY-SPINACH SALAD

Serves 6

Sweet and tangy strawberries complement creamy avocado in this spring green salad. The dressing is a surprisingly
delicious blend of flavours, including strawberries, basil, garlic, chives, honey and mustard.

INGREDIENTS
SALAD

65–75 g/2½–3 oz round lettuce, cleaned and torn into bite-size pieces

65–75 g/2½–3 oz spinach, cleaned and torn into bite-size pieces

350 g/12 oz whole strawberries, washed and hulled

50 g/2 oz celery, chopped

2 tbsp chopped fresh chives

40 g/1½ oz pecan pieces

2 avocados, peeled and cubed

DRESSING

4 large, hulled strawberries, puréed

120 ml/4 fl oz vegetable oil

30 ml/2 tbsp white wine vinegar

1 tbsp chopped fresh basil, or 1 tsp dried

1 tbsp chopped fresh chives

1 garlic clove, finely chopped

¼ tsp prepared mustard

5 ml/1 tsp honey

¼ tsp salt

¼ tsp freshly ground pepper

DIVIDE THE LETTUCE and spinach among six bowls. Top with the strawberries, celery, chives, pecans and avocado.

Combine all the dressing ingredients and mix well, preferably in a blender or food processor.

INDEX